Twice Blessed

Learning to Live and Love Again

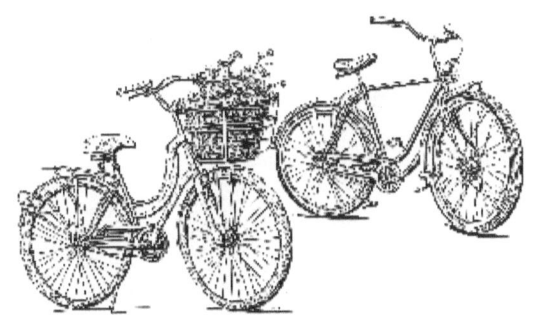

Twice Blessed

Learning to Live and Love Again

by Charlaine Martin

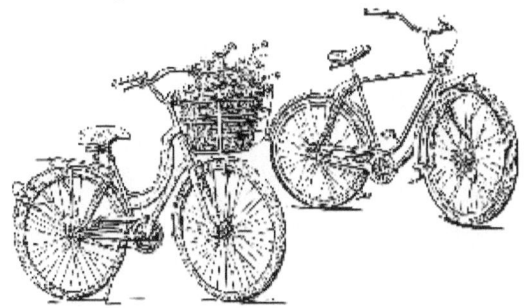

take heart books

Twice Blessed *Learning to Live and Love Again*
All Rights Reserved ©2025 by Charlaine Martin

ISBN: 978-1-958818-15-2 (paperback)
Library of Congress Control Number: 2025927603

Published by
Take Heart Books LLC
Toledo, OH

take heart books

Cover art from Canva

The chapter *"Two Valentines = Doubly Blessed"* is a revised version of *"The Last Valentine's Gift"* which first appeared in *Live & Learn: Unexpected Lessons from God's Classroom*, published by 3G Books. Used with permission.

Bible Versions used are The Holy Bible, New King James Version (NKJV) Copyright 1982 by Thomas Nelson.

The Holy Bible, English Standard Version (ESV), Text Edition 2016. Copyright 2001 by Crossway Bibles, a publishing ministry of Good News Publishers.

*Names have been changed to protect the privacy of the individuals involved. Also, some situations have been slightly altered to maintain the privacy and integrity of the individuals involved while staying true to the story.

In loving memory of Don Engelhardt,
My high school sweetheart and First Blessing,
and
in loving honor to my Boaz,
my sweet Squirrel and Second Blessing.

Table of Contents

Introduction

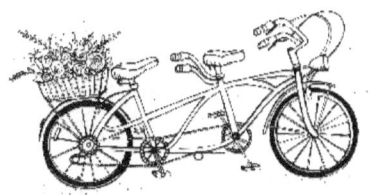

W hen my husband died, I was left to seek help and support independently. Once I found a church to attend after his ministry ended, people were not very helpful because they were busy trying to "fix" my grief. No one seemed to accept that grief is an ongoing process. After the funeral, everyone expected me to move on when the "casserole train" ended. I failed trying to work through it alone, so I sought help.

My quest led me to four different books, one of them written from a secular viewpoint. I found some books on mourning from a Christian perspective helpful, but none addressed the full spectrum of my grief journey. How can other Christians left behind when their spouses die from long-term terminal illnesses possibly grieve their loss and navigate their new lives alone? Other people's stories of their grief journeys helped me see how they worked through it and found a place where they could function again in their new lives. That question churned in my mind, which led me to write *Twice Blessed*.

While writing this book, I was shocked to learn how many people receive devastating medical news. The American Cancer Society, in 2023, reported 1,958,310 new cancer cases, with 609,820 cancer deaths in the United States.[1] Of non-cancerous diseases that can cause death, 10 to 15 percent of people with lupus die early due to disease complications.[2] The mortality rate for people with multiple sclerosis is 75 percent, primarily due to complications.[3] Heart disease is the

1   Rebecca L. Siegel MPH, Kimberly D. Miller MPH, et. Al., "Cancer statistics, 2023,"CA: A Cancer Journal for Clinicians, 2023;73(1):17, abstract on PubMed, accessed April 26, 2025, https://pubmed.ncbi.nlm.nih.gov/36633525/.

2   Daniel J. Wallace and Bevra Hahn, Dubois' Lupus Erythematosus and Related Syndromes (8th ed.) (Philadelphia, PA: Elsevier Saunders, 2012), as cited by Lupus Foundation of America, accessed April 26, 2025, https://www.lupus.org/resources/lupus-facts-and-statistics/.

3   Marisa Wexler, "MS Tied to 75% Increased Risk of Mortality in US Study," Multiple Sclerosis News Today, June 13, 2022, https://multiplesclerosisnewstoday.com/news-posts/2022/06/13/ms-tied-75-percent-increased-risk-mortality-us-study/.

leading cause of death in the U.S., claiming the lives of 2,500 people from cardiovascular disease every 34 seconds per day.[4] This information shows that many other diseases can cause progressive premature death. I found that information staggering when I read it. There certainly has to be a tremendous number of Christian couples who face these illnesses every year.

My thoughts then turned to how I could use my experiences to help others in this situation. Anticipatory grief began when my late husband was diagnosed, which is an essential part of healing. I wanted to help widows and widowers discover, from that initial sting of diagnosis, how terminal illness forces a couple's life to change forever, and they can indeed navigate their new lives. I also found it valuable to share how facing loss and deciding whether to remarry are reasonable considerations, not only those issues but how grief transforms from pain to joy-filled remembrance years after the funeral. Moving on is an important aspect of healing from grief since God has a wonderful plan for your remaining years on the earth.

My dilemma became what would be most valuable for you in your grief journey? When my husband died, I discovered that not only was he gone, but I had lost our hopes and dreams, the continuity of our family ties, our daily routine, our traditions, and my personal identity in us once intertwined with him. A large part of me died, too, which I found disorienting. By sharing these stories with you, I hope to help you identify portions of your grief and encourage you to take it to God in prayer while allowing the Holy Spirit to help you work through those pain-filled places. You can use the For Reflection sections and related Bible passages at the end of each chapter to help you process your experiences by prayerfully considering your own story. I'm confident you will eventually accept how God brings joyful hope into your life again.

Some situations I lived in, like being a pastor's wife and fitness professional, put me in the public eye. You may or may not relate to them, but some readers will. Also, being a chronic illness warrior and

---

4   Connie Tsao, MD, MPH, FAHA and Seth Martin, MD, MHS, FAHA, 2023 Update, American Cancer Society. Lewis, Cathy. The American Heart Association, Newsroom, "Heart disease remains leading cause of death as key health risk factors continue to rise" https://newsroom.heart.org/news/heart-disease-remains-leading-cause-of-death-as-key-health-risk-factors-continue-to-rise. Published January 27, 2025. Accessed May 6, 2025.

mother of young adult children who grieved along with me made these a unique combination. Maybe you are like me, and you find yourself forced into the spotlight, shutting down your emotions in front of people, tabling your grief. It's not uncommon.

Maybe some situations wore you out. They did for me. I believe for other pastors' spouses with adult children under public scrutiny and those with health conditions, this is likely true. Chronic pain and fatigue made caregiving difficult, compounded by inadequate sleep, which many of you will likely testify occurred to you if you were in a similar situation. There are several places in *Twice Blessed* that you might relate to and others you might not. Your story is incredibly unique. I hope you will chronicle yours.

My prayer is that you will have several ah-ha moments to help you connect with my caregiving and grief journey so you can view your pain through the lens of God's Word to find healing. Hope can be found by reflecting on different grief points of this bittersweet God adventure. You can come through it with gratitude for the new life God has for you. May you find that same hope as you discover His work in those moments. He has been with you the entire time. He still is. I hope *Twice Blessed* will help you cling to the Lord during your healing journey so your mourning will turn to dancing[5]. May He bless you with an abundant new life and maybe, if it's His will, love again.

---

5   Psalm 30:11-12

Chapter ONE

The Diagnosis Hits Hard

Just like clockwork. Ralph, an elderly gentleman, swam laps at noon every day, where I guarded the pool at the YMCA. He popped his snorkel mask off his face, dumped a small amount of water from it, and then perched it on his bald head. This eighty-something guy looked up as I rounded the corner carrying my rescue tube and hailed me over like a taxi driver. Pensive, he leaned against the pool wall to rest between his swim sets and inquired, "Why would God give your husband, one of His servants—a pastor—cancer?" His gaze fixed on me as he wondered how I would handle this trial. He admitted, "I'm not a religious man. I hope you don't mind me asking."

"It's okay for you to ask questions," I assured him as I kneeled on the deck beside him to avoid causing him neck pain. Considering how best to answer his question in a way that would make sense to him, I decided that what Don said to someone else with the same question would be best, "Why not? Don doesn't feel that he's more special than anyone else. After all, the Bible says it rains on both the just and the unjust alike.[6] And he was right.

Considering our discussion, the swimmer, submerged to mid-chest in the water, responded, "Hmm. Thank you. I appreciate your honesty." Then, he placed his mask back on his face and resumed his swim workout while he pondered my answer.

***

The mail arrived, and my husband spied a particular envelope and plucked it out of the stack. He opened this important letter, ripping across

6   Matthew 5:45

the top neatly with his sword letter opener.

It was the test results from the doctor's office. Stunned, we read: "Diagnosis: Colon Cancer Stage 4."

"Oh, my!" I gasped, holding my face in my hands. Don stood frozen beside me as the color drained from his strong face. Shaking his head in disbelief, he re-read it, both of us hoping he had misread it. No mistake. There it was in black and white. Tears welled up in our eyes as we held each other. We got the horrific news no one wants to hear.

We received the bad news on Monday, right after our son and his new bride were married on a chilly, rainy Saturday in April. "When do you think we should tell the kids?" I asked Don while we ate dinner after work. Sipping my diet cola, I wondered about his thoughts on the timing. I felt certain that surgery and treatments would begin soon, so we needed to tell them before that time.

He laid his fork down on his plate, glanced out the window, and considered my question. "We can tell the girls this weekend, but let's wait until Seth and Rebekah return from their honeymoon. I think they said that they plan to come home Saturday." His usually bright eyes now looked lackluster as he pondered their possible reactions.

"I agree." I set my drink down while my eyes remained fixed on him. "They don't need this dark cloud hovering over their first days together." He nodded in agreement. We told our girls the same weekend. Our youngest was a senior in high school, set to graduate in May. Our older daughter was a young adult who lived nearby. They responded in shock, tears, and loads of questions. "How bad is it? Are you going to die?" Our heads spun in a whirlpool of overwhelm. We could barely wrap our brains around it since we had many unanswered questions. This adventure started what seemed like the proverbial "hell on earth."

Don, my childhood sweetheart, was only in his mid-forties at the diagnosis. He served as a bi-vocational pastor in a small struggling church, shepherding this loving, aged congregation for more than thirty hours a week. But then, he also worked a second job at a local plant for forty plus hours a week. His physical work at the plant made him muscular. I still see his square jaw, easy smile, and kind blue eyes framed with gunmetal-rimmed glasses. He looked quite pastorly with sandy, brownish-grey hair that hedged his balding head. I found it hard to accept his diagnosis because his level of illness didn't show. Many people we knew were shocked when they learned he had cancer.

I supported his pastoral ministry as the Christian education director at our church. I also worked for a local YMCA as a part-time instructor in the pool and fitness center to help with our tight budget. Our kids, who attended the local schools, helped tremendously in the work of our church. Two had sprung from the nest, and the last one was ready to leave home. Fatigue was our norm. Bi-vocational ministry and church renewal drain the energy out of these pastors and their wives, even during joy-filled ministry. With cancer added to the mix, we discovered a new level of exhaustion. Doctor appointments and more tests dominated our crammed calendar.

I could see the worry in his eyes when he came home from the surgeon's office and shared his colonoscopy pictures with me. This thing in his body looked like a monster from some grade B horror movie pulling all the power lines to gorge upon. It demanded a vast supply of hemoglobin with a road map of blood vessels flowing toward it. As it hoarded this vital life source, it caused the internal bleeding his doctor discovered in routine testing through Don's employment at the plant. The softball-sized tumor settled into the outside of his colon near the appendix—no wonder he didn't have typical symptoms.

He had no blockages causing problems. Hemorrhaging occurred outside the colon wall, so no blood showed up in his stool to tip his doctor off. He also didn't experience the associated pain. For this reason, his cancer was diagnosed at stage four instead of earlier. We thought the seventy-to-eighty-hour work weeks drained him, but he was also anemic. Apparently, it amplified his work fatigue.

How Could This Happen?

This menace grew silently over ten years. As we thought back, we realized several things could have caused it. One is Don's previous work as an engineer with heavy metals in investment casting. It was a time before they knew the risks of the materials in his industry, such as cobalt, zinc, and asbestos. Some of his managers had gastrointestinal problems that plagued them since they had worked in the labs with those same materials.

Or it could have occurred later when a crop duster dumped farm chemicals in the field beside the parsonage of our first church while

Don mowed the lawn. I pulled a bedsheet off the laundry line behind the parsonage while he mowed and the kids played on the swing set. Out of the corner of my eye, I noticed a crop duster plane on the horizon headed our way. In a nanosecond, I yelled to the kids, "Run into the house *now!*" They quickly darted indoors. I waved my arms to get Don's attention, but the mower's engine drowned out my voice, "Don, get inside!" I ran inside and shut the door, thinking he heard me. I waited to let him in, but I popped out again when he turned the tractor for another pass. I stood anxious but had to protect the kids and myself. Suddenly, he realized I'd called him, but it was too late as he started dismounting the riding mower and dashed toward the door. That toxic cloud engulfed him as the plane buzzed the field, unloading farm chemicals on the crops. *How could that pilot be so careless?* I seethed. Once he reached the door, I let him inside, warning our children to stand back.

We were amazed, shocked, and angry all at the same time. "Didn't you see the crop duster? Didn't you hear or see me try to get your attention?" Peering at him in worry, I had him strip down in the laundry room and throw his clothes directly into the washer. I reached into the folded laundry to pull out something he could put on to go take a shower.

"No, I didn't until he'd already started dusting. I must not have heard you, but I saw you make the kids go inside. I wondered what that was about until I saw the crop duster come down and you pop out the door."

"What kind of issues could come from that man's careless disregard for us?" I muttered. *Could he have breathed in those chemicals? What you breathe, you can also ingest.* Aggravated about the whole incident, I dumped the laundry detergent and softener in, slammed the door shut, and then brusquely started the washer.

***

Don's family history warranted watching him for possible heart attack and stroke. My meat-and-potatoes guy had high blood pressure at about the same age his father did. Since Don's father died of a heart attack in his fifties, that possibility lurked in the back of our minds. As a personal trainer, I kept watch of his food when I shopped and prepared meals. I also urged him to exercise, which he did sporadically with the physical demands of his work at the plant. We never imagined he would be diagnosed with a terminal illness like cancer. Never in a million years.

As his wife, I walked this scary road with him from beginning to end. Our children had briefly been involved with his medical care and transportation while I worked. Reflecting on that time, I'm grateful they didn't have to fight alongside him for the entire four years. Our tiny congregation blessed us by providing support whenever they could through prayer, meals, checking on our kids while we had to be at the hospital, and so much more. However, I still had limited respite.

A Visible Witness with an Invisible Illness

God used this horrible time in several ways. First, he worked in the hearts of people who observed us, seeing how we would handle this battle with cancer. Our atheist neighbor, a childhood Holocaust survivor, wished us luck and once offered some "plants," which he grew to help ease his pain. I cringed because I didn't want to know anything about his "plants," which were illegal then. Don smiled and politely declined, "My pain is well managed. Thank you for your concern, though." We later learned that Peter was impressed by our faith and steadfastness as a family through it all.

Don led many people through prayer and shared the gospel for them to consider, most of who would never set foot inside a church. He probably would never have reached them for Christ if he had been healthy. One individual was a young man Don eventually baptized in the pool at the YMCA. God works through some circumstances that are difficult to understand yet are effective for the kingdom. Our situation may have been one of them.

As a fitness professional and pastor's wife, I've witnessed numerous cancer and terminal illness stories through church attendees, gym members, and clients. Shock, disbelief, and anger are all common responses for couples hit with the sudden realization that terminal illness is an unwanted intruder in their lives. Of course, no one ever wants nor expects that kind of news. But it's a scary reality these days.

THOUGHTS ON THIS CHAPTER

Why did you choose this book to read? Chances are you didn't find it by accident. Either cancer barged into your life, or you minister to families struggling to cope with cancer. Perhaps another terminal illness has caused your search. I pray that our story will help you see God's work in your situation, recognizing His amazing love in your life. Romans 8:28 NKJV says, "And we know that all things work together for good to those who love God, to those who are the called according to His purpose." People tend to use this passage in a trite manner. There is nothing good about terminal illness nor the struggles you both must endure. So, I don't offer you this passage as a spiritual Band-Aid. Instead, I believe God can turn your situation into an opportunity for beauty to emerge from the ashes of your pain. What you and your Sweetheart have experienced can be used for a greater purpose.

Grief over long-term terminal illness occurs in stages throughout the process, like what we endured amidst cancer. Some of my grief continues even now, several years after Don's death. Ironically, we had walked alongside others through their cancer, but it was our turn. It certainly was harder living through these steps ourselves.

I want to share how God's loving hand can actively guide you and your healthcare team. Maybe you celebrated the five-year cancer-free milestone or a long remission of debilitating illness together. However, God does not abandon His children left behind by the death of a spouse who lost the war with a terminal illness. The good news is that when you are in Christ, there is a victory for you and your Sweetheart when they enter the pearly gates and for you as you continue here on earth. There can be life and love, God willing, afterward.

For Reflection

These are steps we experienced with excerpts from the story you can consider as you think about the diagnosis of a terminal illness in your story:

» Shock—We couldn't wrap our brains around the harsh reality of Don's diagnosis.
» Denial—I couldn't believe he had cancer since he looked fine.
» Anger—The possible causes shocked, angered, and overwhelmed us all at the same time.

Questions for Reflection

1. Describe the moment you and your Sweetheart received the initial diagnosis of their illness.

....

....

....

....

2. What steps did you experience when the diagnosis came? If your spouse has passed away, reflect upon the time of diagnosis and the feelings both of you had then. How did you respond?

....

....

....

....

3. Did you have help in the initial stages of diagnosis and treatment, or did you have to go through it alone?

....

....

....

....

4. How did your family respond when you told them? How did their responses affect both of you?

....

....

....

....

5. Have you been able to see how God showed up during this time? What did He do or impress upon you and your Love? Were you angry with Him? About your situation?

....

....

....

....

Scripture for Reflection

Here are some suggested Bible passages you can read prayerfully. Feel free to journal your thoughts about each one as it relates to your story:

• Matthew 7:24-29

....

....

....

• 2 Corinthians 12:9

....

....

....

• Matthew 11:28–30

....

....

....

What other thoughts or Bible passages come to your mind?

....

....

....

....

Chapter TWO

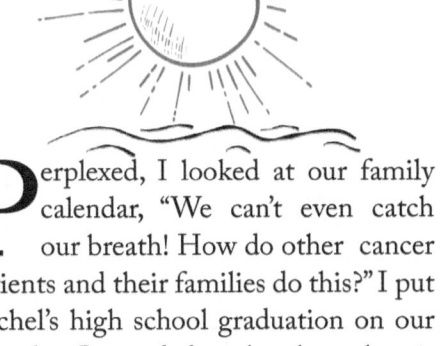

The Dizzying Treatment Maze Begins

Perplexed, I looked at our family calendar, "We can't even catch our breath! How do other cancer patients and their families do this?" I put Rachel's high school graduation on our calendar. It needed to be there, but it felt like a major achievement to avoid a schedule conflict with Don's treatments.

"I'm sorry," Don apologized as he realized how much his appointments took over our lives.

"Hon, there's no need to apologize! It is what it is. You need these appointments. I'm trying to find a way to make everything work."

There's no doubt about it. Entering the healthcare maze was mind-boggling. More appointments for doctors, surgery, and chemotherapy dominated our lives. This new schedule became a cruel dictator telling us what we could and could not do.

Don met with a surgeon to review his case immediately after the news. Dr. Ellis, a blond-haired, middle-aged man, welcomed us into his office to discuss the procedure he would use to remove the right side of Don's colon. Sitting across from him in aqua office chairs, we watched as he pointed to a surgical diagram. "I will make an incision from immediately below your sternum, straight down, go around your naval, and then down to the top of your pubic bone. Because the tumor is above the appendix and because you are in stage four, I'll remove the entire right side of your descending colon to barely pass the appendix. Next, I'll connect the intestines like this. Then, I'll give you a temporary ostomy so you can heal properly. After your follow-up appointment, we will schedule another surgery to close the ostomy site."

We numbly listened, unable to comprehend everything we heard. Don's surgeon went on, "I'm hopeful that we can get a clean margin of the tissue from the immediate area, meaning there would be no remaining cancer cells." Little did we grasp that some significant changes would begin in his body. It was more than we anticipated.

Dr. Ellis rested back in his seat and looked compassionately at us, "Lovemaking doesn't have to end because of all you will endure. There are still ways to be intimate with each other."

I felt heated embarrassment rise in my face but remained silent. I struggled to believe I heard the surgeon bring this topic up.

Holding my hand, Don replied, "We realize that. Thank you, though, for caring enough to tell us." I could see him blush, too, glancing in my direction and then back to his doctor.

***

The surgeon was a kind man who, I found out later from a mutual friend, knew the Lord. Jean, who also worked at the Y with me, queried, "Who's Don's surgeon?" after she heard about his surgery and the hospital where it would be done.

"Dr. Ellis," I responded, keeping my eyes on the lunchtime swimmers, the rescue tube resting comfortably under my arm, my swimsuit and guard shirt damp. We had just finished the children's swim lessons, and Jean had her towel wrapped around her waist.

She exclaimed, "Oh, I know him and his wife. They go to my church. His wife has paraplegia. They experienced significant changes because of a car accident that confined her to a wheelchair." It made sense now why this doctor believed we needed to know about these adjustments we'd have to make along the way.

And we certainly did. A time came much later when lovemaking as we knew it ended. When this happened three years later, we lay in bed intertwined as we mourned our loss.

Navigating New Territory

Don's abdomen and chest began to look as if he'd got caught in a knife fight and lost. It disturbed me since he'd never been through any surgery before, and now several surgeries were done over a short time.

He acquired several new reminders of his battle with cancer. Ileostomy and colostomy scars appeared like parking spots on one side of a route on a GPS with a roundabout halfway circling his belly button and with the end destination at the pubic bone. Medical ports bumped up under the skin, having been installed, removed, and reinstalled over time, leaving short, angled dashes below his collarbone on each side. The other major scar was from a liver resection, just under his rib cage and down one side, which I'll share about later.

One night, cuddled in bed, I ran my hand across the soft hair on his bare chest as we kissed, and I continued gently ruffling it with my fingers. We gazed into each other's eyes, smiling with affection. My hand wandered slowly down toward his belly. Suddenly, he gently grasped my wrist. "Careful, please," he cautioned. Startled, I pulled my hand away. I'd become caught up in the moment, but he reminded me that he was still healing from his latest surgery. With a whispered sigh, I rested my hand back on his chest. Neither of us liked these limits. We struggled to accept his harsh new bodyscape.

How Did We Get Here?

Tired from all the blood draws and vitals taken in the middle of the night at the hospital, Don quietly asked me, "Would you help me clean up and put on a fresh gown? No one has done that today."

Shocked, I said, "What? You've got to be kidding!" I couldn't believe it. The time was 7:00 pm, after I got off work. "They should have done it this morning. No worries," I assured him.

Unbeknownst to us, the hospital where Don stayed was severely short-staffed and preparing to close. I'd never seen such medical sloppiness in any hospital.

I roamed his room, gathering a basin, soap, washcloth, and a new hospital gown. He cautiously got out of bed, pivoted, and then sat in the tall-backed beige chair at his bedside. I pulled the curtain around his space for privacy. The warm, soapy water was a fresh relief from his body's stickiness and pungent odor. I could see he appreciated my washing him rather than a stranger. He held a bed pillow to his abdomen, leaning slightly forward with a wince. His back was easier to clean without a surgical wound. Once he was dried, we got his blue-dotted gown on him. He relaxed back.

"Did they change your bedding? It looks filthy and stained. Oh, my! Someone left a needle from your blood draw on here!" I couldn't believe what I found. I pointed it out to the nurse at the central station, who seemed unfazed by it. If I hadn't changed Don's bed sheets after helping him bathe, he would have lain in filth for who knows how long. *How do they get away with this?* I fumed. Dr. Ellis wasn't sloppy, either. Certainly, these conditions had to be unusual in hospitals, so I was very protective of him.

***

When the surgeon started talking about Don's discharge from the hospital, I couldn't wait. Still, I had to prepare our house for his recovery. I stood in our bedroom looking at our waterbed, trying to decide where would be best for him to sleep and recover. *Hmmm, there's no way he can sleep here. Those padded wooden sides and the waviness of the mattress would make it impossible to get in and out without ripping his stitches. How about the sofa?* I continued into the living room to inspect it. **Sigh* this won't work either. I wish we had a spare room, but we don't. This pitiful sofa has to go.* It was so worn, we'd stuffed pillows into gaps and then covered them with a cheap throw blanket. *That broken spring would poke through everything and jab him. We can't risk it.* We were so unprepared for this part of his cancer treatment.

Nothing we had at home would work, so I asked our kids to help me assemble a sturdy, comfortable futon. I bought one at our local discount store and drove it home in our minivan. "Okay, let's get this inside." We reached for the box corners but found ourselves in a wrestling match created by its enormous, awkward-sized flimsy box while trying to get it into the house. "It's too much for us. What should we do?" I asked them, grasping for answers.

"How about asking Hank or one of the other men from church?" my son offered.

"Good idea!" With renewed hope, I called around. Hank, more than happy to help, came over with his tools and helped us set it up.

"I can see why you called!" he chuckled. Skillfully, he put it together while I held parts in place. In no time, it was up. Then we put the tattered sofa on the curb for trash day.

"Thanks so much!" I said with gratitude.

"No problem! I'm glad I could help. Let me know if you need anything else." He packed up his tools and drove away.

With the futon in place, I ensured that Don had plenty of pillows and a foam wedge to make himself comfortable with his personal nest. *Hopefully, this arrangement will work.*

Well, it did and didn't. At least Don had something he could sleep on that wouldn't swallow him up, stab him, or cause his incision to pull open. But he did have a tough time getting up and down, and he couldn't prop himself up as well as I imagined. "Thank you, Char. I appreciate all you, the kids, and Hank have done to make me comfortable." He did his best to make it work.

LIVING IN A STRANGE NEW ENVIRONMENT

Chemo sessions started after the surgeon released him from his care. The convenient office location made our trips manageable. The first time entering the chemo clinic, we found it odd to see patients with bald heads, some with hats or bandanas, happily munching crackers and sipping ginger ale as they watched their favorite shows on their individual televisions. These people, on the same journey as Don, relaxed comfortably in recliners hooked up with tubes pumping chemotherapy medications into their bodies. Some of them dozed off during the three-hour infusion time.

Staff members cheerfully chatted with patients in the clinic's soothing yet upbeat atmosphere. My husband, quite the extrovert, spoke with anyone about anything they wished. As a result, he found a captive audience to share Christ's love and compassion with patients frightened about their futures. We could see God moving in their hearts, and we prayed for them often.

Since appointment times were during the day, Don had to take some time off from his job at the plant to go for treatment. It seemed that most of the cancer clinic patients were now on disability. Our children helped take him there and home when I had to work. Shocked, the doctors and nurses couldn't believe he was still working. "We can schedule you for next Tuesday at 9:00 a.m." The young woman at the scheduling counter peered at him with a questioning look through her pink-framed glasses.

Oh, I'm sorry. I can't make it before 3:00 p.m. on weekdays because I work. What do you have in the evenings or on weekends?" He leaned against the counter, fatigued, as he flipped his pocket calendar open.

Eyebrows raised in surprise, his oncologist, Dr. Green, walked up to pass paperwork to the cashier. "You aren't on disability yet?"

"No, sir." Don directed his response toward his doctor.

Glancing toward the scheduler as a couple of patients filed past us, he stated, "Please, set standing appointments for Mr. Engelhardt on Wednesdays at 3:00 p.m. and Saturdays at whatever time works between his schedule and ours."

"Thank you so much!" Don's stress gave way to relief.

The young woman kindly handed him a card with his monthly appointments.

When Don informed all of his medical team that we have a saying at our house, "No work, no eat," they got the point. If he missed too many work hours, we couldn't pay our bills, including co-pays or deductibles. We rearranged our schedules as best as possible to get him to his appointments, taking off as little time from his job as possible. Don's employer also found ways to accommodate his chemo schedule, especially since it was a standing appointment time.

***

Don came home with a chemo pump pack during his weeks of infusion therapy. We began to understand why some couples needed separate beds or rooms. I found it difficult to fall asleep with the whirring and clicking sounds it made, so I picked up some earplugs on the way home one groggy day. Then, another morning, he caught his pump tubing on the headboard of our bed in the dark, heading to the bathroom. "Ouch!" I heard his disgruntled voice as he shuffled toward the door. It was the beginning of our exhausting, demanding schedule of treatment.

Don cycled on and off chemotherapy treatments to beat down the cancer that still resided in the liver. Another surgeon removed a tumor and some surrounding lymph nodes, which appeared later. However, he still needed surgery to deal with the three smaller tumors spread out in both lobes and the dome of his liver.

We trusted these doctors could cure Don by this point in his treatment because they claimed they could. We heard about all the advancements in cancer treatment, so it seemed plausible. He was young and otherwise healthy, so his body should bounce back from the surgeries and treatments.

We were angry with this beast called cancer as if it were an entity all its own. "Lord, I hate cancer!" I cried out one day with tears streaming down my face as I rammed the sweeper under the dining table. I took my frustration out on dust and dirt as if they stood in cancer's place. I poured out my heart to God about how I despised what it was doing to Don. I have to say that our home was the cleanest it had been for a while.

I was furious about the possible causes too. God had taken us through so much before, and we trusted Him to take us through this deep, dark valley too. Hopeful and determined, we continued forward with the recommended treatments.

COPING WITH THE CHANGES

This surgery was the first of several that forever changed his body. I'll never forget the first time I saw Don's new scar roadmap after the surgery. He showed me the staples on his long abdominal incision as he lay on his futon, "Goodnight, Hon. I love you." I kissed him and went to bed. This was my husband's belly, but it didn't look like it. It was unsettling. Peeling blood-soaked gauze from the seeping wound and replacing it with new bandages wrenched my heart. My husband became my patient.

Don felt self-conscious about his scars. People stared at him when he came to the YMCA to aqua jog. I suggested, "Honey, wear a t-shirt or tank top to cover the scars." It seemed like a plausible solution. Don found it difficult to rotate from his torso because it pulled the scar tissue. He had to pivot his whole body to get something from beside or behind him. Sometimes, I would have to get what he needed instead. These permanent changes took getting used to.

Chemotherapy was a whole different ordeal for us. While its purpose was to kill cancer cells, it also killed healthy cells. *How barbaric!* Don's lips, fingers, and toes turned bluish as the chemo effects accumulated in his body. That bothered us too. Bluish-purple is never a good skin color for anyone—*ever*. He fatigued sooner, so we became frustrated doing some of the activities we wanted to do, such as taking long walks together. Also, he needed to nap more frequently. Maybe he didn't sleep soundly from the chemo pump's whirrrr-click-click sound going off throughout the night.

One of his meds caused a pins-and-needles sensation in his hands when he touched anything cold. If he drank a cold beverage, it could make him feel like his throat was closing. Don had to bundle up more often, which he was not used to. Usually, he was a warm person who preferred wearing short sleeves in the winter. Nausea settled in, and his tongue had a horrid film that made food taste bad. Strong cinnamon candies were his companion to cover the awful taste in his mouth.

Another chemo medication caused a terrible rash, so the doctor gave him steroids before treatments and Benadryl after. I reconsidered his meals and the type of clothing he wore. We also kept gloves around for him to wear when he knew he would have to handle something cold. I even got him a medical alert tag in case of emergencies. My sturdy, independent man had become more fragile than we wanted. Life forever changed for us.

CLEARING AWAY GLOOM

I noticed depression settle over him like a dark cloud. He began to talk about dying, expressing concern about what would happen to me after he was gone. At this point, the doctor hadn't said he was terminal. Instead, the medical team was very hopeful they could cure him. So, I encouraged him to write a five-year plan for his life to counteract this dreariness in his soul.

"Why five years?" he quizzed me, baffled by my suggestion.

I hoped to encourage him. "Because the possibility of a cure for you is stronger than the possibility of your dying from this," I said. "Besides, there is a five-year survival window before they consider you permanently cancer-free. So, what would you like to do or see over the next five years?"

With great thought, he started making his list: see all three of our children married, see our grandchildren who weren't born yet, ride a motorcycle, and go on a nice trip together. Those things were very reasonable, so I encouraged him to pursue them. What a change to his morale! We kept his list on hand so we could refer to it often. Then, when he felt crummy, he would look it over.

THOUGHTS ON THIS CHAPTER

Surgery and the disease's accompanying treatments affect the patient's body, and these changes concern couples. Depression is common for both the terminally ill patient and the caregiving spouse. One may be optimistic, while the other expresses doom and gloom. The healthy spouse is more likely to be able to re-focus than the ill spouse who is enduring physical trauma. Talking with your pastor or a licensed Christian clinical counselor to process your emotions can help if these memories are too much. Disease-related support groups are also available around the nation.

It's very discouraging when there seems to be no future left. But, even if the illness you or your Love faces is terminal, as long as the ill spouse is alive and able to have conversations, God still has a plan for them.

I thought of Paul in prison with Silas in Acts 16 and how the jailer was saved. Don had an audience with people every chemo session to share Christ and His love. God has worked, or will work, in your situation too. It's also important to consider what someone with a terminal illness might like to see or do and make it happen, if possible. This joint venture of doing things on that "bucket list" keeps couples talking intimately, dreaming, and working side by side. As you had dreams together before illness, you need something to look forward to more than ever. If your spouse is gone, was there a way you helped them keep hope alive as long as they lived? If not, it might help to identify any remorse over what you did or didn't do for them, offer it up to God, and then let it go. You can't change the past.

For Reflection

Below, I share the steps I went through dealing with changes and treatments and the corresponding quotes from this chapter:

» Loss—We lay together mourning the loss of intimacy and the new changes we faced.
» Trauma—I became protective of Don and found it hard to change his bandages. He became very self-conscious about his scars.
» Adjustment—There were many changes we had to make from his bed after surgery to foods and temperatures due to his chemotherapy.
» Anger—I vilified cancer and targeted my anger at it for what it had done to Don.
» Determination—The doctors' encouraging prognosis made it easier to press forward with surgeries and treatments hoping to cure him of cancer.

Questions for Reflection

1. What treatments were used for your loved one? How did that affect each of you? Your family?

....

....

....

2. What did, or would, you do to help give your Sweetheart a reason to wake up each day? If not, what would you do differently?

....

....

....

3. What blessings did you notice at this time?

....

....

....

Scripture for Reflection

- Hebrews 12:1-2

....

....

....

- Deuteronomy 31:5-7

....

....

....

- Proverbs 3:5-6

....

....

....

What passages or thoughts come to you right now?

....

....

....

....

....

....

....

....

....

....

....

Chapter
THREE

God Lifts Us Up When Plans Fall Flat

I t would've been nice to think everything would go according to the plans Don's doctors set. Twists and turns came our way, and we weren't prepared. Yet, we could only express gratitude for God taking over when He redirected our course.

Dr. Green, Don's oncologist, reviewed his case just before attending an oncology conference with a surgeon, Dr. Matthews, from Ohio State University Hospitals. After hearing him speak on newer treatment alternatives for colorectal cancer, Dr. Green asked for his thoughts about some of the obstacles he faced with Don's case. "Would this patient be a good candidate for radio wave ablation?" Dr. Green inquired over coffee in Dr. Matthew's office.

"Well, if what you are telling me is correct, he certainly could be. Refer him to me, and I will gladly examine him to determine if this procedure would be right for his case," Dr. Matthews replied, confidently offering his business card. So, at Don's next appointment, Dr. Green shared this discussion with Dr. Matthews with us, and recommended that we meet with this oncology surgeon in Columbus.

With this glimmer of hope, we traveled to Columbus to explore this exciting possibility. We wanted to learn more about procedures that might be available to beat down or eradicate the lesions in Don's liver. Sadly, though, we discovered radio wave ablation was not an option. Dr. Matthews explained, "You have lesions spread throughout your liver. The best course of action would be a liver resection for the area with the majority of these cancerous lesions.

I can remove up to seventy percent of your liver. It would regenerate over six months to one year, depending upon the amount removed. Your recovery time would take about six months. However, I need to remove 60 percent to get a clean margin. Then you would follow up with chemo with your oncologist at home to deal with the remaining lesions." His professional demeanor also contained a level of friendliness that felt genuine and confident in what he could do to help Don.

We looked at each other, stunned. "What do you think about this?" Don directed his question to me, looking for insight I wasn't sure I possessed. I listened intently, but I didn't understand everything discussed.

Thoughtful yet hesitant, I responded, "It's up to you. Your body would be going through extensive surgery and recovery. If this is what you believe best, I fully support you." He set the surgery date, and then we discussed what we had learned on the way home.

Friends and church members helped us muster funds together so I could stay in Columbus with Don during his surgery. "Char, please take this to help with your travel expenses. This won't be cheap or easy. We want to reduce your stress so you can focus on Pastor Don." Margarette, a sweet, plump older woman in our church, handed me a check for one hundred dollars in a card.

"Thank you! But, are you sure?" I worried about her because she lived from check to check on social security.

She replied, "I took up a collection in Sunday school class," as if reading my mind. "We want to help you."

"Aw! Thank you so much!" I accepted the check and hugged her. I couldn't help but shed a few tears of appreciation.

I went home and reserved a room at an extended-stay hotel in Columbus, not far from the hospital. It had a kitchenette so I could make meals in the evenings. What I didn't realize was that not only would I have to stay one week, but it turned into two. Although it was cheaper this way than staying in a motel, our funds were extremely tight, even with financial help. I sat in the surgical waiting room, glancing over at the progress board occasionally. It took a bit longer than the doctor told us, but he finally came out in his surgical scrubs to tell me how it went. "Don's surgery went textbook perfect," he announced with a tired smile. "I did indeed remove 60 percent of his liver from one lobe, and we have a clean margin." I felt so relieved. Don had approved beforehand for the liver segment removed to be used for colon cancer research. His surgeon recommended we follow up with Dr. Green after returning home for chemotherapy to tackle the remaining lesions.

RESTLESS, YET NO REST

"Char, do you see an orange frame around the dry-erase board?" Don asked me sounding somewhat confused. Unfortunately, recovery took a nasty turn after he moved into his room—the anesthetic caused crazy hallucinations. Several times, he saw weird orange frames in his line of vision. Since his room was private, we wouldn't bother anyone, and no one would bother us.

"No, Don, there isn't. It has a light wood frame," I replied, wondering what caused him to see something strange on the nurse's communication board.

Later that night, he thought he had to get up and go to work, among several other anesthesia-induced scenes running through his brain. I lost so much sleep the first two nights, simply trying to keep him in bed. "Don, you don't have to go to work. It's okay. You get to sleep in." I sprang up quickly to prevent him from getting out of bed. Even though it had an alarm to alert the nursing staff if he arose, moving much could be dangerous. The incision ran just under his ribcage from one side to the other, then slightly down the other side. He looked a bit like an anteater with a nasogastric tube inserted through his nose and taped in place along with intravenous tubing and wires to record his vital signs. If he fell, it would be a disaster.

Recovery became even more complicated. In addition to the hallucinations, awful, gut-wrenching hiccups shuddered Don's body, causing breathing difficulty. Oh, what a challenge! He also began throwing up greenish-brown goo tinged with blood. The healthcare team and I wondered if we were going to lose him. Don became despondent and wondered the same thing.

One caring nurse took me aside in the hallway and said with concern etched into his brow, "He's really down and seems to have lost hope. He needs you to cheer him on and encourage him. You are critical in his recovery process." *How could I do that when I was not very hopeful myself?* I wondered. Exhaustion and pain colored my outlook and distorted reality. Somehow I succeeded, though. The Holy Spirit must have stepped in for me.

Mother's Day came during the sleepless hiccup period. I kept family, our church, and friends informed about what was happening by sending out prayer requests online. Prayers from around the globe held me together and continued for Don's recovery, which looked bleak to me. Our kids sent me Mother's Day e-cards. It was tough to be joyful; I slumped down in the recliner in Don's room and cried. *Happy Mother's Day, indeed!*

UNEXPECTED SUPPORT

Funds drained quickly, eaten up by parking garage fees and hotel charges. I tried to spare our money by not eating food at the hospital. Most of the time, I skipped meals until I returned to my hotel room. Gluten-free, dairy-free protein bars sustained me on several occasions. Still, I didn't have enough money for another week.

Don's mom insisted on calling me numerous times every day. I imagine she needed to connect with him somehow, even if it meant wearing me down on the phone. The first night of his hiccupping fits and hallucinations, I got no sleep. I trudged to my room early in the morning, hoping to catch a few winks when my phone rang. Instead of patiently talking with her, I bluntly informed her, "Mom. I've been up all night. No sleep. I can't talk right now. I'm going to bed for a while." I think I hung up on her mid-sentence, but I don't recall.

Later, I remembered some friends who lived in the Columbus area. I contacted them to let them know about Don's cancer and that he was in the hospital. They invited me to stay with them when they learned about my situation. Their spare room was a Godsend. They even gave me a key so I could come and go. When I came back at night, we talked and prayed together. God provided for my extended stay with these wonderful friends who supported me tremendously.

The day of his discharge finally came. A bubbly young nurse came in with cheery news, "You get to go home today, Mr. Engelhardt!"

In his now raspy voice left by the nasogastric tube, "I'll be ready when the wheelchair comes!" His incision had begun to seep clear fluid, so a couple of nurses heavily bandaged him for the long trip home. I gave him some of my overnight maxi pads to catch the seepage through the bandages in the car.

When the time came to leave the hospital, it was a harrowing experience driving Don to our home, almost three hours away.

Fibromyalgia fatigue complicated my drive. My body hurt, my brain fog refused to clear, and I worried about fighting sleep partway home. Usually, I could barely handle driving one hour at a time due to exhaustion and pain. It morphed into a grueling, nerve-racking drive. Every bump made me nervous as he groaned or yelled, "Ouch!" while he held his belly pillow to his abdomen. I apologized profusely, but he assured me, "It's okay, Char. You're doing great. You can't dodge every bump or pit in the road."

When we pulled up in front of our home, I could barely stand upright, let alone help him into the house. His abdominal muscles couldn't help lift his foot onto our stoop, so he put one arm around my shoulder while he held his belly. His shirt had tell-tale damp spots where seepage soaked through the bandages. We stepped up together as I gently lifted the back of his leg to place his foot on the step, finally making it inside. I had asked one of our kids to put sheets and pillows on his new futon ahead of time. He held the belly pillow in place to cushion the jarring as he sat down.

Once his pain settled, I carefully helped him remove his damp shirt, changed the outer bandages, and put a fresh, clean, oversized shirt on him. His face, pale from the excruciating pain he endured to this point, began to relax. I retrieved a glass of water from the kitchen so he could take his pain meds and carefully helped him lie down for a nap. "Thank you, Char." I kissed him on the cheek. This spot became his home for the next couple of weeks. My boss graciously allowed me ample time off work to tend to his recovery as well as my own.

God provided so much for us during this trying ordeal. The Lord provided the money we didn't have and a place to stay when I had nowhere else to go. I also received support and encouragement from his fantastic medical staff, family, and friends. God carried us on eagle's wings.[7] He provided so much for Don through my ability to be there with him, hospital staff whose care went above and beyond, friends and family who dropped everything to visit him, not to mention holding his belly together the entire way home. It was all God's work.

---

7   Isaiah 40:31

THOUGHTS ON THIS CHAPTER

When a situation goes from bad to worse, we tend to think that God has forgotten us or cave into our fear. These reactions shut us down when we can't afford to let this happen. Just when our Sweethearts need us the most, we must be available. They are already overwhelmed by the abrupt changes to their bodies. Our faith in God's loving care for us, both the caregiver and the patient, becomes the wings that carry us through the challenges that confront us. The best place to begin is by prayerfully looking up relevant Bible passages in God's Word. Your pastor or a hospital chaplain can help you find what you need.

SPECIAL CONSIDERATIONS: PONDERING FAMILY MATTERS

In times like this, your marriage and family ties are tested. It will either tear you apart or draw you closer. For us, it drew us closer. It also became a bridge among distant family members, which built stronger family connections. Our kids were more aware that their dad may not be with us someday. They visited us more intentionally, especially during holidays and special occasions. They could see the immense value of their relationship with their dad rather than simply taking it for granted that he'd always be here.

One of the most strained relationships can be with your loved one's parents. The mama bear or papa bear instinct comes out badly, wanting to protect their child from harm and make everything better. If your relationship with them is strained, they might treat you like you stand in the way of their son or daughter in distress. Dementia and other memory issues for elderly parents likely compound these stresses. They don't understand everything that's going on. Whether your relationship with your in-laws is strained or great, understanding their needs and meeting them in small ways go a long way in helping them with their grief.

You've likely faced family members' responses. Sometimes, they behave uncharacteristically based on how you've perceived their personalities. Others become overly helpful and cause difficulty without meaning to do so. Some become know-it-all busybodies offering unsolicited—and often unsound—advice. At the same time, others will behave as if your Love's funeral is tomorrow. These types of responses can zap your energy and strain relationships.

Unfortunately—yet fortunately—you became the point person for your spouse. Maybe you needed to buffer their responses by simply stating, "So-and-so asked how you are doing." When you think about how pulled apart you were because your spouse was someone else's somebody—a son or daughter, father or mother, brother or sister, and so on—it puts it into perspective. Your love for them, along with God's strength, was a vital bridge to maintain healthy relationships. The best things you could do were extend grace, ask forgiveness for your offenses, and overlook any hurt they caused. You need each other more than ever.

God often uses tension for growth. Sometimes, what we think is "their" problem may be our own. Prayerful reflection and asking God to show us our weak spots help free us of resentment. This big step prepares us for our future life without our Sweethearts. All the more, God's plans will prevail.[8] We can remove obstacles to that growth by trusting God's plans and purposes for us.

FOR REFLECTION

Steps we went through dealing with Don's sudden turn and change of circumstances:

» Trusting God's Provision—We had to scrape funds together and I went hungry most of the time while he was in the hospital for surgery. Some friends invited me to stay with them when I let them know he was in a hospital near them.

» Overwhelmed—I lost a lot of sleep the first two nights after Don's liver resection trying to keep him in his bed.

» Loss of hope—Don began to lose hope while he struggled with the liver resection. I struggled too wondering if he would make it.

» Trusting God in weakness—I could barely handle driving one hour at a time, but God carried us home.

---

8   Proverbs 16:9

Questions for Reflection

1. How did your Sweetheart's surgeries and treatments affect both of you? How did they handle it?

....

....

....

....

2. During times you could barely manage the challenges you faced, how did you see God work? In what ways did He show up during these times?

....

....

....

....

3. How did family and friends respond to your spouse's surgery and treatment process?

....

....

....

....

4. How did you handle tense situations with those who've caused stress for you and your loved one?

....

....

....

....

5. What changes would you make if you could have a do-over?

....

....

....

....

6. What circumstances did God use to draw you to Himself during tough times?

....

....

....

....

7. What pulled you together as a couple?

....

....

....

....

....

Scripture for Reflection

- Isaiah 40:10

....

....

....

- 2 Kings 4:1-7

....

....

....

- 2 Corinthians 9:10-11

....

....

....

....

What other passages stand out to you? What makes them special during this particular time in your terminal illness journey with your Sweetheart?

....

....

....

....

....

....

....

....

....

....

....

....

....

....

....

....

....

....

....

....

....

Chapter **FOUR**

RESCUED!

"**G**et to the emergency room now!" Don's doctor ordered. Thankfully, he was between breakout sessions when his doctor called. He found me at the book table I had been browsing in the foyer. "Dr. Matthews called me back. No cancer! But he said the pain I've been having when turning my head is probably a blood clot in the jugular vein. I have to go to the emergency room."

Stunned, I laid down the book I intended to purchase. It no longer mattered. "Okay. I'll take you right now."

For about three weeks before this event, intense pain in Don's neck worsened. "I'm fine," he assured me, brushing off my concern. It was difficult to turn his head without tremendous discomfort by this point.

"Maybe you should call your doctor and ask him about it," I suggested. However, in his stubbornness, he declined.

Finally, after hearing his constant complaints, I insisted, "Talk to one of the nurses between the conference sessions." *How frustrating! Why does he keep ignoring it?*

This suggestion sounded reasonable, "Okay, Char. I will."
It's about time!

GOOD NEWS, BAD NEWS

We expected some of his test results a few days before the conference, but for some reason, they were delayed. When Don's cell phone rang during one of the breaks between sessions, he was glad to hear the doctor's office finally had his test results. So far, the cancer had not returned. That was a tremendous relief. The timing couldn't have been better because he gave in to my pressure to talk to his doctor about the neck pain. "While I have you on the phone," Don asked his oncologist, "I am having a horrible pain in my neck. It's hard to turn my head. Is this something to be concerned about?" Then his doctor ordered him to go to the hospital immediately. This conversation turned our lives upside down at a most inconvenient time.

ANOINTED TIME

June was the time for our denomination's annual conference. Almost a year after his liver resection, Don, as all pastors were required, attended the general sessions where decisions were made for denominational and church issues. These servants of God could gain greater knowledge and spiritual growth from the continuing education sessions offered to lead their churches more effectively. Some of the pastors' wives and church delegates also attended. It was a great time to catch up on friendships and encourage each other as well. We always enjoyed being a part of it. However, this year turned out to be different.

"Before we head to the hospital, I need to let Dr. Woodward know and see if I can do a brief version of my presentation." Don slipped into the auditorium while I stood near the door, peaking in with my car keys in hand. Church delegates and pastors grabbed coffee and water, filing into the auditorium past me for the session reports.

As the afternoon session began, Dr. Woodward called the meeting to order from the podium and announced Don's emergency. "Pastor Don Engelhardt, from Hilltop Chapel, needs to go to the hospital with a medical emergency. Would you come forward, Pastor Don, and all our pastors and elders present? Let's lay hands on him and pray for his healing."

Dr. Woodward pulled a vial of anointing oil from his suit coat pocket as all the men moved to the front, surrounding Don. He said, "God's Word tells us that if any of us is sick, we should go to the elders that they pray and anoint us for healing."[9] They each placed a hand on him with reaching heavenward. "Dear heavenly Father, Your servant is ill. Please, in the name of Jesus, give him complete healing. We love You and thank You for what You are about to do. May Your name be glorified in this situation. In Jesus's name, amen."

"Pastor Don will now give us a brief report about Hilltop Chapel

9   Paraphrased from James 5:14

before he leaves." Dr. Woodward stepped away from the lectern so that Don could take the mic.

"Thank you for allowing me to do this quickly," Don said, letting the delegation know God's work in and through our tiny congregation that had begun to grow. Afterward, he briskly made his way to the car, with me following behind him.

***

Don's neck pain was indeed a blood clot in the jugular vein caused by his medical port pressing on a corresponding vein. In emergency surgery, the attending physician removed the port on the left side of his chest. Later that week, the doctor installed a new one on the right. Don was given blood thinners to dissolve the clot.

While Don recovered in his room, I was concerned he would nick himself shaving, so I told him as I put my purse on my shoulder, "I'm going to the store to get an inexpensive electric shaver for you. You might cut yourself with your regular razor and have a difficult time stopping the bleeding."

"You're overreacting," he chuckled, reclining on his bed.

I didn't see it that way, "Sorry. I disagree. Always err on the side of caution, I say." I gave him my *I'm Right* look and a kiss before heading out the door. He knew better than to argue with me. So I bought the shaver, which he much later thanked me for getting when he struggled to groom himself.

Pulled Apart

We were stuck three hours away from home. Our youngest daughter, Rachel, had stayed behind because of her college classes and work. In our absence, her car broke down, causing concern for all of us. I felt so torn about where I should be. I couldn't be in two places at the same time, with her and with Don. I also couldn't handle the three-hour drive each way because fibromyalgia limited my drive time to only an hour at a time. Don needed me to be the wife by his side. Rachel needed me to be the mom taking care of her. He felt bad that he couldn't fix her car for her like always. So, while Don was relaxed in bed, he called one of the gentlemen from our church to help Rachel with her car troubles. We were grateful he could, and a couple of the ladies checked in with her. I felt better but still felt weighed down with guilt.

Our regional director for Ohio and his wife invited me to stay at their home. They ministered to me during that rough time. Limited finances prevented me from getting a hotel room during Don's impromptu hospital stay. Their invitation meant so much to us. I visited with Don in the hospital during the day; at night, I'd go back to their home to share what was happening, and they prayed with me.

God's timing was perfect for dealing with the blood clot. Don had me with him where he needed me to be. The Lord also provided help and safety for our youngest daughter and looked after my needs. God does take care of His servants' needs.

ON TRIAL

A couple of years later, we received God's miraculous intervention when Don participated in a clinical trial in Bethesda, Maryland. Meteorologists predicted that a blizzard would cover the region from Western Pennsylvania to Washington DC. A retired couple from our church in Pennsylvania was concerned about our ability to drive home through that storm. They understood the limits my health put on me, as well as how chemo and cancer affected their pastor.

Don's cell phone rang while we were at the National Institute of Health. This couple pleaded, "You shouldn't drive in the storm that will hit hard tonight. Let us come get you. Where can we meet on your route?"

Don assured them, "We will be fine. We've driven through some nasty snow squalls a number of times."

But the persistent former school teacher took charge, "No, we insist! The drive could be treacherous. Let us meet you at least part way back." So, we relented.

Sure enough, the blizzard hit with a vengeance. White-out conditions made visibility almost impossible on the highway. "Wow! This blizzard *is* bad," my body tensed. We pulled into the restaurant to wait for them and a church friend of theirs who wanted to accompany them. There was no way either of us could handle the drive as exhausted as we were.

We got into their van's back seat and chatted along the way. The traffic crept along at a snail's pace. The three-hour drive wore on for six tense hours as we occasionally crept past some cars stuck at the side of the road and a couple of jackknifed semis.

One foolhardy truck driver hauling an empty flatbed decided to pass us in the left lane of the divided four-lane highway. The roads were extremely slick, which caused his flatbed to slide toward our lane as he tried to pass us on the left. My heart pounded in my throat at the sight. We prayed while the flatbed barely missed the glass beside Don's head. *Lord, don't let this trailer hit us!* The back corner slowly slipped past, mere inches from the window, when it suddenly stopped, stuck in the snow on the side of the turnpike. It was as if an invisible hand alongside the van's window prevented the trailer corner from ripping through the glass and hitting Don. We all thanked God, breathing a sigh of relief. God cared for us in visible ways, revealing Himself to us and others around us. He used these events to remind us of His compassionate love for us later when we desperately needed it.

THOUGHTS ON THIS CHAPTER

God's guiding hand took control of incidents that we didn't realize had the potential to be life-threatening. One of them definitely could have cost Don his life. The other would have been disastrous, but I'm unsure of the potential outcome. For whatever reason, God had a specific plan for Don through these events.

It would be easy for us to get caught up in the stresses of cancer treatments with other incidents during the battle. Please know that we occasionally struggled, but we were frequently aware of God's activity in our situation. If we take the time to consider how God, our Creator and Protector, is working in situations, our pain mingled with fatigue melts away. We were amazed by God's marvelous work. It is so important to give God the glory regardless of the outcome. Our spiritual health depends on it. Others around us will also take notice. I invite you to use the time to see God at work in your situation.

FOR REFLECTION

Some of the steps I managed to deal with during these harrowing situations can be found below:

- » Stunned—When Don told me about the need to go to the emergency room, I was shocked.
- » Frustration—I knew Don needed medical care for his painful neck, but convincing him was the difficult part.
- » Conflicted—I felt so torn about where I should be, with Don or Rachel. I felt guilty that I couldn't be with both of them.
- » Protective—I knew that blood thinners would make it difficult to stop bleeding if Don nicked himself with his razor blade. He could also get a nasty infection. I bought him an electric shaver for safety.
- » Overwhelmed—I could see the potential for the flatbed trailer to rip through the glass beside Don's head and hit him. All I could do was pray.

Questions for Reflection

1. What scary situations did you encounter as your Sweetheart's illness progressed?

   ....
   ....
   ....
   ....

2. Were there any remissions that gave you a sense of false hope or conflicts you faced?

   ....
   ....
   ....
   ....

3. What emotions did you feel in this stage of your Sweetheart's illness?

   ....
   ....
   ....
   ....

4. How did God take care of you and your Love during your trials?

   ....
   ....
   ....
   ....

Scripture for Reflection

*   Isaiah 55:8-9

   ....
   ....
   ....

- Jeremiah 17:7-8

....
....
....
....

- Philippians 4:6-7

....
....
....
....

- Romans 12:12

....
....
....
....

Do you have any other thoughts on this chapter or Bible verses that come to mind?

....
....
....
....
....
....
....
....
....
....

Chapter FIVE

Grasping at the Wind

I'm sorry. I can't release those records of your test results. You have an outstanding balance with us," the records clerk informed Don.

"But we've consistently paid twenty-five dollars a month on our bill. I need those records for my new oncologist in Pittsburgh," he pleaded.

"Our billing office informed you that you must pay one hundred dollars per month to be in good standing with us. Now, if you pay the balance of your tests with our collections specialist over the phone, or pledge that you will begin paying one hundred dollars monthly, then we can send them. They can help you clear this issue up to release your records," she flatly stated.

"I'll see how we can get that balance to you, but we definitely can't pay more each month. Somehow, we have to eat too." Don sighed, looking in my direction.

"Thank you for calling. Have a good day."

He hung up, looking downcast. "For a Catholic Charities hospital, they aren't very charitable. How can we pay what they require?" he said. "I'll see if the oncology office can help."

I walked up to him at the breakfast table and wrapped my arms around him. "God's got this somehow."

The big wave of storms pulled us under after we began ministry at our new church in Pennsylvania. Yet God worked continually in the background, taking care of things ahead of us. Interestingly, we never received Don's lab results from that hospital in Canton, Ohio, before our move. This oversight was intentional since we couldn't meet their demands for one of his visits there. We discovered they withheld the critical findings that would have clued us in on the storm brewing quietly in his body. We pledged to pay them fifty dollars each month, which we took out of our grocery budget.

At least we could hold back the collection hounds, but they were certainly unhappy about it. They claimed we didn't qualify for financial assistance through Catholic Charities, who owned the hospital. Yet, our youngest daughter qualified for financial aid for her college tuition due to her dad's cancer. This discrepancy made no sense.

Taking Shelter from an Impending Storm

Don's new oncologist ordered tests rather than fight to get them from the hospital in Canton. We had shared with the pastor search committee that, as far as we knew, Don was cancer-free. But was he? That question had haunted us. We soon knew.

"I'm sorry, Mr. Engelhardt, but your tests show that your cancer is back—and your cancer markers are through the roof!" Dr. Feldman looked at him with sympathy as he sat on his stool near his laptop computer. Discouragement hit us hard. Don sat on the exam table, leaning into his hands on the edge, staring at the floor. The doctor continued, "Since these findings show high cancer markers, we need to be aggressive with your treatment."

Saddened by this news, Don nodded in agreement. "Let's do it."

That raging monster came back with a vengeance. The lengthy delay aided the cancer's silent growth. It re-emerged in Don's liver with a small tumor at the base of his pelvis near the tailbone.

Don underwent yet another liver resection. I could barely breathe, knowing what he went through with the first one. I fully expected him to go through the same frightening aftermath. However, his recovery this time went far better than the first. Although God had not healed him as we thought, we found a ray of hope.

News of the Forecast

"Gentlemen, I'm sorry to inform you, but the cancer is back in my liver and now in my pelvis." The elders' quiet concern showed on their faces at this revelation as they sat around the meeting table listening to their new pastor. These men were no strangers to cancer and the devastation that comes along with it because they lived in a cancer hotbed.

"What will this mean for you?" Don's head elder, Jim, inquired. "We can get pulpit supply for you when you need to be out. Please update us as soon as you know when you must be away from the pulpit. We will step up to the plate to help out as well."

"I'll have to be out for six to eight weeks, but we can still hold meetings after I get home if you don't mind meeting in my living room," Don offered.

"Pastor, let's take it one step at a time. We can adjust as the need arises," Jim said. The church leaders probably felt misled about their new pastor's health status but rallied behind him. Don talked with me after the meeting, "I appreciated their tremendous support. But why is God allowing this setback?"

"Honey, I don't know. We have to trust God, though. He didn't bring us here for no reason." He nodded in agreement.

This news triggered another storm in the church's underpinnings. While Don lay in the hospital recovering from his surgery, the church council president-pastor relations-treasurer—a man with too much control of the church—conducted a survey that caused tensions and dissatisfaction within the membership. This survey set the stage for a major firestorm threatening our ministry's effectiveness. Yet Don never failed in his pastoral commitments.

God's Shelter in the Prevailing Winds

We routinely traveled to Pittsburgh for doctor's appointments. Still, we were grateful that chemotherapy treatments were conveniently located in a nearby town. Don found a new ministry audience, including Dr. Feldman and other cancer patients, with whom he could discuss faith topics.

"So, Mr. Engelhardt, what do you think God is doing in your situation? I don't know much about Christianity, but I'm curious how your beliefs affect your thoughts on this new twist in your cancer journey." Dr. Feldman sat on his rotating stool, awaiting Don's reply.

"I know it's no accident that I'm here now. I often wonder what God is doing in the background, but I trust Him in this situation." Don sat on the exam table with his hands folded in his lap.

Dr. Feldman sat with one arm across his midsection, his chin resting on his gently held fist in thought as he listened. Then he responded,

"You sound hopeful, which is good. Having a positive attitude in negative circumstances is on your side. It can make all the difference in how your body responds to your treatment."

Every visit brought more questions about Don's Christian faith in adversity. It seemed that God opened up these conversations with his Jewish oncologist.

This unique platform for ministry helped him reach people in our new community too. There were a couple of church members who'd been recently diagnosed with cancer as well. When Don visited them in their homes and the hospital, people who overheard his conversations with them got a glimpse of God's love during challenging times. Nothing is ever wasted with God.

***

It wasn't long before it became apparent to Don's oncologist that his cancer was terminal. However, Dr. Feldman seemed to hold on to hope for him since he was still young, and Don's faith kept him hopeful.

"You've outlived the protocols for this type of cancer. To be quite honest, we aren't sure exactly how to proceed. The current chemo meds aren't effective anymore, and you're allergic to one of the primary chemotherapy drugs used. Would you be interested in participating in a clinical trial?" The doctor rolled his seat away from his computer, waiting for Don's reply.

Sitting on the exam table, Don leaned on the front edge, pondering this new option as he listened to more information about clinical trials in general. He looked to me for support as I sat across from them not knowing what to think or say.

After a thought-filled moment, he sighed with his eyes fixed on his doctor, "Sure. Why not? I have nothing to lose at this point. If it helps me, great, but if it helps someone else, it's worth it."

"Okay, I will look for what fits your type of cancer."

Resignation clouded Don's dulled eyes. By this time, his once muscular shoulders now looked spindly, as if belonging to a man in his eighties, not someone a year shy of fifty. His belly protruded from surgeries because scar tissue threaded through his abdomen like spaghetti, weaving his intestines tightly together. As we left the clinic, Don silently walked with his clear Lucite cane. His mind seemed like it was a million miles away. We felt shaken, pondering what God was doing in the background on our long, silent ride home.

Within a couple of weeks, Dr. Feldman recommended a phase II trial designed to train the immune system to attack colon cancer. He appeared to be a great candidate since his cancer was a textbook case, and Don held up well despite all he had endured. Trips to the National Institute of Health in Bethesda, Maryland, took up residence on our calendar.

Cancer On Trial

After his intake interview, the trial team accepted Don at this national medical research center. We learned that as a phase II trial, they were looking for dosing, more side effects, and which cancers and stages it would be best suited to treat. Would this clinical trial work? No one knew. What if it didn't? We mulled over so many questions. Traditional therapies no longer worked, and his medical team had to dose him with antihistamines and steroids to manage his allergic reactions to one of the chemo drugs. We wanted God to use this new direction for his healing so badly. But would He? Skepticism and guarded hope hovered over our family. Several surgeries and chemotherapy treatments since Don's diagnosis of colon cancer about three years ago failed to cure his cancer. Would our hopes be dashed yet again?

***

We had a series of hoops to jump through at the treatment center. Several security checkpoints greeted us due to 9/11. Security guards searched our vehicle and bags while we got out and entered the security station. We placed our bags, wallets, and other small items into plastic bins that went through a scanner on a conveyor belt. A security guard scanned our bodies with a wand as we stood still. We handed them our driver's licenses while they printed out temporary name badges. Security checks lasted for what seemed like an eternity. Finally, they cleared us to go through the gates. "You won't need to go through this level of screening now. Simply show us your badges each time you visit."

"Thank you," we replied as we returned to our car and drove to the correct building.

At Don's first appointment, the trial team kindly assured us that if there were complications or if his cancer became worse, they would stop the trial and recommend he see his primary oncologist at home. Every two weeks, he needed injections of a vaccine designed specifically for him from his blood serum. The scheduler gave him a regular appointment slated for three months at a time, and the information we needed for his future visits.

Blood work and vitals were standard fare every visit. The team needed a CT scan for the first time to give them a baseline view of the cancerous tumors present in his body. When meeting with the trial doctor, they would check symptoms and read the test results. "Mr. Engelhardt, your cancer markers are drastically higher than what your oncologist reported. Your CEA count from your oncologist's report three months ago, just before you started this trial, was 332. It is now 1,335." She stood with his chart, sounding apologetic for giving him bad news.

These cancer marker numbers shocked us. Don, wide-eyed, exclaimed, "I can't believe it! How did it get this bad?" He reached over and took my hand.

"You're not disqualified from the trial at all," she assured him." You can leave the trial and seek traditional treatment at any time. You are in excellent condition compared to the patients we usually see. You are able to walk in on your own, and your other vitals look good." The doctor pulled out a pad to write down his next appointment date and time for the scheduling counter.

At least it was a glimmer of hope in this raging cancer storm. Don wanted to find out if it could help him, so he agreed to continue. "Okay, I'll do it then. If it doesn't help me, maybe my participation will help someone else." He sat forward in his chair with his arms resting on his thighs.

***

We wandered through a maze of hallways and a list of stops on our way to the day hospital for his injections. Our written directions provided a map through the research center. Otherwise, we would've undoubtedly become lost. When we entered the room, a line of recliners for patients greeted Don. The vaccine formulated from his blood serum had been sent down from the pharmacy for the nurse to administer.

"I will inject the vaccine at the front side of your armpits and groin. Afterward, we want you to wait an hour before leaving to watch for side effects. You may feel tenderness at the injection site. We need to know if you develop a rash, fever, or flu-like symptoms. I'll be back then to see how you are doing. Do you have any questions?" the pleasant nurse asked.

"Not right now," Don replied. She gave him his injections, and then we sat and read for an hour. No side effects! So they cleared him to go home.

We came two weeks later for the same tests and treatment, but no CEA or CT scan. Although our spirits were not as high as initially, we still hoped that Don could benefit from this trial.

However, Don's third trip to NIH was a much different story. He felt tremendous pain both sitting and walking and had trouble emptying his bowels. We noticed at Thanksgiving that something wasn't right. "Maybe I ate something that doesn't agree with me," Don said as he held his very distended abdomen, attempting to tame his discomfort.

"I'll give you more brothy soups and less fibery foods," I offered. Although it helped some, Don still felt terribly bloated.

He was plagued by a fever that would come and go over the two weeks, and it was present on this visit. His pale skin felt cold to the touch. Pain forced him to walk hunched over his cane. He was gaunt, with his belly protruding more prominently. I had no clue what to do for him except support him or get him something he might need. I felt so helpless.

He flinched when I touched him, yet he yearned for touch, one of his love languages. Instead, I let him reach out to touch me as needed. At least he could control what type of touch he received and when. Don had lost ten pounds over those last two weeks because he could barely eat without feeling nauseous.

His oxycodone prescription ran out, so sitting for long periods tortured him. As we sat in the waiting room, we discovered his appointment time had been changed without any notice. But the lead contact person got him in to see the team anyway. This event turned out to be a blessing in disguise. They admitted him to their hospital promptly.

LOSING OUR GRIP

Stressed, we listened as his team told us Don's cancer had worsened. Don groaned at this news. With deep disappointment, he nodded in agreement with their diagnosis. I felt despair with him.

"The tumor in your pelvis, which we've known about for a while, has grown and is now causing a partial blockage. It, along with the swelling of your abdomen from the distention, is pressing on the nerves and blood supply to your lower back, hips, and legs," the resident doctor explained. "We may need to put in a stent to open your bowel or do a colostomy to relieve that pressure. We will discuss this with your medical team at home to determine the best course of action," his clinician informed him.

Don had struggled with basic tasks at home due to his symptoms. The medical staff gave him medication to dull the pain and sedate him. As he drifted off to sleep, I watched him. *How in the world does he deserve this mess, Lord?*

GOD'S GRACIOUS PROVISION

The NIH social worker tried to get a room for me at The Lodge on campus, which makes it possible for patients' families to stay on the campus near their loved ones. However, no rooms were available. So, she gave me a list of hotels with special rates for patients and family members. I chose one as close as possible because not only could I get lost in a box, but I could also get lost with our GPS in this city.

I missed a couple of turns, which wound me through a housing development. The GPS said the destination was on the right when it was actually on the left. *Ugh!* Finally, the large hotel sign out front welcomed me. By the time I arrived, my nerves were frazzled. Fibromyalgia fatigue and brain fog added to my detour. My body felt bruised all over, clouding my thoughts. I wanted so much for us to be home by now, but I was grateful for the friendly hotel staff who went above and beyond to help me. I desperately needed a good night's rest.

In the morning, packing what I would need to catch the shuttle back to the hospital, it dawned on me why God had provided extra money family and friends had given us for travel and lodging.

Several people from our church pitched in to reduce our financial burden. I had received a check in the mail from someone we didn't even know. It made me wonder at the time why money came. Now I knew. Since celiac disease and problems with dairy caused extra challenges, I always had to pack my own food. This time, I had over-packed. Don thought I was paranoid, but it proved to be the right decision. Our car acted as a freezer for my meals that frosty January. The Lord ensured we had precisely what we needed for Don's extended time in the hospital, so far from home.

I worried about what kind of bill we would receive because this stay would add to the mountain of medical debt we already owed. I asked the admissions person to whom I should give our insurance information. She gave me a blank stare. I repeated, "Who should I give our insurance information to? I want to make sure we take care of this promptly."

Finally, it dawned on her what I meant. "Oh! There is no cost to you," she assured me. "He was admitted during a clinical trial, so it's included. But it's also paid for by your taxpayer dollars." *Awesome! Thank you, Lord!* I rejoiced in my heart. The last thing we needed was another expensive bill. God kept taking care of us over and over. Don felt relieved to know all was well for us in the middle of this situation.

We had already faced many trials in which God acted swiftly on our behalf and provided for our needs. It was as if our Abba Father God pulled out his wallet and said, "Don't worry, my children. I've got it covered! Don't you worry about a thing." Although we felt stretched spiritually and emotionally, we learned we could also trust Him in this storm.

God also gave us wise, caring people to guide and direct us and make sure I was okay. He rerouted me when I got lost. Don didn't have to worry about me; he just had to focus on getting well enough to go home.

THOUGHTS ON THIS CHAPTER

What storms have you faced already? As stressed as you probably were, hanging on to God's promises while looking through your faith history, can you see that you could count on God to carry you through everything you faced? Trust that He loves you and your Sweetheart infinitely more than you can imagine.

FOR REFLECTION

The steps we took to deal with the reoccurrence of Don's cancer were:

- » Disappointment—We often felt disappointment with each bad report in this segment of our journey.
- » Dejection—We felt deep disappointment and overwhelm, like all of the bad news would lead to his eventual death. I wondered why this would happen to him, God's faithful servant. He certainly didn't deserve all of this bad news, and I felt helpless in all of it.
- » Cautious hope—We had seen God's hand this far, but the bad news made us feel cautious. We hoped with guarded hearts.
- » Trust in God—God kept taking care of us over and over. Don felt tremendous relief to know all was well for us in the middle of this situation.

Questions for Reflection

1. What steps did you experience at a similar stage of your spouse's terminal illness?

2. How were your finances impacted, and do they affect you now?

....

....

....

....

3. How had God provided the funds and resources that you needed with your Sweetheart's medical care?

....

....

....

4. Did your Sweetheart go through clinical trials or experimental treatments? How did this affect you?

....

....

....

....

5. If your Sweetheart has passed away, reflect upon when you thought their illness was in remission, but all you could think was, "Oh, no. Not again." What were your thoughts at that time?

....

....

....

6. Looking in your "rearview mirror," how did you see God working in your disappointments and harrowing situations?

....

....

....

....

Scripture for Reflection

- James 1:2-6

....

....

....

- Mark 8:22-26

....

....

....

- Philippians 4:13

....

....

....

- Isaiah 12:2

....

....

....

What thoughts about this part of your roller coaster adventures come to mind right now?

....

....

....

....

....

....

....

It's possible to give gratitude to God in your memories of disappointment. If you are ready, you may find it helpful to pray something like this:

Lord, I felt like You abandoned us as if You didn't care. Yet, as I think back to when I realized my Love wasn't healed and that they might go sooner than I wanted, I want to thank You for taking care of us. Forgive me for my selfish doubt. Thank You for Your faithful love, enduring patience, and constant provision. I don't know how non-believers can go through situations like this without You. I am so glad I am Your child. Amen.

If you can't pray like this because you still hurt too much, you can share your heart with God about this time in your journey with your Sweetheart. Come back to Him and pray as often as you need. It's an important part of your healing. God loves you deeply.

Chapter SIX

Distorted Views of Healing

Sweat trickled down the evangelist's ebony face as he fervently preached and prophesied. Suddenly, he called a woman forward by name who he didn't know before this healing service. "Gina, come forward, please."

She obediently came to the front of the church and stood before him.

"I detect that you are afflicted with a tumor in your abdomen. This cancer is not from God! Sister, be *healed* in the name of Jesus!" He placed his hand on her forehead, and she immediately fell back into the waiting arms of some men standing behind her at our friend's church.

"Praise You, Jesus!" and "Amen!" rippled through the stifling, packed sanctuary with the crowd spilling out the open doors. Don sat, intently watching as we listened to this highly respected traveling evangelist-healer. *Lord, is there healing for Don here tonight?* I remained cautious, not desiring to press God for what I wanted. I didn't doubt God could heal my husband if He chose to do so. But I did question the authenticity of this man on the platform because so many had been exposed as charlatans.

On the platform, this man of God continued to invite whoever wanted healing to come up to the altar, calling out, "God has healing for you if you would just receive it!"

Don couldn't stand up at the altar, so he rested his head on his hands poised atop his cane and prayed. He could barely handle walking to this church just two doors down from the parsonage. Besides, he came for his friend who desperately wanted Don to be cancer-free. The doors and windows stood wide open, allowing a gentle evening breeze to refresh this standing-room-only crowd. People had witnessed healing before and had seen prophecies play out that this evangelist proclaimed in the name of Jesus from his previous visits.

Another woman stood up and testified of the healing she experienced after her last visit to this church, when the evangelist proclaimed healing for her the previous year. All the people in our community who knew her and of the ailment that tormented her witnessed her miraculous transformation. She faithfully followed the evangelist's instructions, and they praised God with her over how God answered these prayers.

Two hours wore on, filled with more prophecies, healings, and testimonies. Yet another person from the line-up swooned after this man placed his hand on her head and prayed over her. She fell into the waiting arms of the men—catchers, for the lack of a better term—who awaited anyone who was slain in the Spirit.

After an excruciating, long time sitting on the hardwood pew, Don's pale face winced. "Let's go home, Char," he whispered. "There's no healing here for me tonight." We stood up and exited the pew. People who had been standing in a doorway nearby quickly filled our vacated spots and continued watching the happenings up front.

Something struck me about this traveling evangelist's words. He shared midway through the service how regional strongholds settle in from a community's strongly held beliefs and can hold them back from God's blessings. He quickly pointed out that they needed to put their faith and trust in Jesus, not him. He'd been there numerous times before performing healings, preaching, and prophesying. He knew they called him back to their church because they looked to him, the wrong one, even though his track record was en pointe for healing and hope. Our hope and healing are in Jesus Christ, not anyone or anything else. It's imperative to keep a proper perspective.

***

I'd be remiss if I didn't address differing views of healing in light of our situation. If you remember, I shared about the lap swimmer who asked me why God didn't heal Don, a pastor serving God. How about our neighbor who had been watching us, an atheist who offered Don "plants" to help him with pain? Both were admitted non-Christians who sought to understand how God could allow his servants to suffer, and how our faith in Christ helped us deal with this challenge. God's love, together with healing, are complex concepts to grasp. We discovered that superstitions and inaccurate ideas about healing abounded both inside and outside of the church.

SIN SICKNESS

A "saintly" woman, considered by many a pillar of the church and community, approached me one Wednesday evening after Bible study with a startling question, "Has Pastor Don repented of his sin yet? That must be why his cancer hasn't disappeared yet." Her syrupy voice nauseated me. This busybody's accusation toward my husband hurt.

I responded carefully, "Nothing more than anyone else. We are all sinners saved by grace. Rather, it seems that God wants to reward Don earlier than us. He must not be done refining us yet."

My answer to this woman, who usually wore her plastic smile, made her scowl and slink away at my correction. Modern-day Pharisees invariably guilt believers who have terminal illnesses in church circles. Her cruelty revealed her heart within this troubled church. How sad this kind of thing happens.

When it comes to critical judgment, this mindset prevailed in Jesus's day. He addressed the same question when He healed the man blind from birth.[10] Jesus stated, "It was not that this man sinned, or his parents, but that the works of God might be displayed in Him."[11] God was indeed glorified through Don's illness and eventual death. Many people around us, Christian and non-Christian alike, told us they were amazed at how well Don held up through surgeries and chemotherapy, keeping a heavenward perspective. They also commended him for his ministry to them and their families in our community, much to our critics' chagrin.

I also brought up earlier how Don had been anointed with oil by the pastors and our denomination's council president. Their particular prayer at the General Conference sessions was for God to take care of the blood clot in Don's jugular vein, which God did. No doubt about it. But another time, Don's pastor friend in Pennsylvania came to a combined community church service with both congregations together for worship. When Sam came forward to take prayer requests at the

10 John 9:1-5
11 John 9:3 ESV

end of the service, he called people forward from the worshippers, "Let us lay hands on Pastor Don and pray over him for healing." He pulled out his small glass vial of anointing oil and asked Don to come forward.

Don had been through this a couple of times and went forward to politely decline, "Thank you, but we've done this before. If God wanted me healed after being anointed with oil and laying on of hands, He would have done so already. Thank you for your loving concern, but this worship service is about Jesus, not me." We trusted that God does physically heal people, but we felt almost as if it had become a circus sideshow. Sometimes, we try to force God to do what we want rather than trusting Him with the manner of healing He chooses for our loved ones.

Well-meaning people had given Don prayer shawls with the intent of God healing him through these labors of love. One year, during the annual conference, Don's mom talked his sister into driving her to Findlay shortly after his liver resection. She insisted that she give him a prayer shawl that she and some ladies in her church made for him. Mom was firmly convinced he would be healed if he would just wrap it around himself. I was frustrated that she kept pressing to get this shawl to him. He was so exhausted from treatment and the grueling participation in conference activities all day. He desperately needed rest.

FINDING GLIMMERS OF HOPE

Desperation showed in her eyes. Looking back at this time, I think she felt powerless to do anything else for her son. If she gave it to him, and he wore it, in her mind, he would be healed. She was firmly convinced of this.

A couple of years after his death, when she lay on her deathbed, I brought it to her. "I think Don would want you to have this now. May you be comforted with it." I carefully laid it over her when she was relatively lucid. I knew it wouldn't heal her, but I wanted her to feel at peace, knowing she'd done everything she could for her son. It wouldn't be long before she would see Don again in heaven.

Now, mind you, not everyone believes the same thing about these lovingly crafted shawls. However, no prayers supposedly embedded in the physical object can ever bring healing. One of our junior high math teachers simply said that as she knit one for him on her knitting machine, she prayed for him. She told us it was a reminder of the prayers that went up to the Lord on his behalf. It was the only reasonable explanation we ever heard. I kept this one since we both had her as a teacher, and it meant more to both of us because of her viewpoint on prayer shawls.

Prayer chains from around the globe circulated Don's name through these groups from the time of his diagnosis to his passing. Some people exclaimed with pride that their prayers worked. However, it was God who answered prayers, not by any power of their own, from all of the people and those who anointed him with oil. God also provided for our needs. He intervened in some serious situations, which extended his life to four years instead of one to one-and-a-half years, the normal life expectancy for stage four colon cancer.

God enabled Don to see his children all married. He held and played with one granddaughter on the floor and met another granddaughter through ultrasound photos. But he never had the chance to meet our other five grandchildren since they were born after he died. God took hold of so many things for us because of His response to these prayers. What's most important to realize is that our prayers are not what caused these things to happen. Instead, the One to whom we pray caused these things to happen. We can't send positive energy or good vibes anyone's way. Rather, we humbly approached the throne of God, pleading with Him on Don's behalf. We had the privilege to come before our loving God, who knows what is best for His servants based on His will.

THOUGHTS ON THIS CHAPTER

The truth is this place is not our home. Don was healed, but not in the way most people expected. The final healing is when we go before the Lord after we die. God rewarded Don early. He was spared of our more recent social challenges and global changes that threaten us today. God says, " I *am* your shield, your exceedingly great reward."[12] It doesn't get any better than that. We will see Him someday when we go into eternity and wonder what all the fuss was about. Be assured that God loves your Sweetheart even more than you do. This life is not all there is.

FOR REFLECTION

Steps involved when confronted by people with false notions of healing:

» Shock—I felt shock when Christians believed the wrong things about Don and how God heals. Didn't they read their Bibles?
» Frustration—I was frustrated with Don's mom pressing to get this prayer shawl to him when he was so exhausted from treatment and participated in conference activities all day.
» Resolve—We trusted that God does physically heal people, but we felt almost as though it had become a circus sideshow.
» Hope—We approached the throne of God, pleading with Him on Don's behalf. We had the privilege to come before our loving God who knows what is best for His servants based on His will.

The false notions of Christian faith-based healing we encountered were:

12   Genesis 15:1 NKJV

» Name It, Claim It—The "name it, claim it" adherents told him that he could be healed if he would just claim the healing because "by His stripes we are healed."

» Faith healers—This man of God invited whoever wanted healing to come to the altar, saying, "God has healing for you if you would just receive it."

» Prayer shawls and other objects—Mom was firmly convinced he would be healed if he would just wrap it around himself.

» Power of pray-ers—Some people exclaimed with pride that their prayers worked.

Questions for Reflection

1. What were some of your own beliefs about healing before this health crisis journey with your Sweetheart began?

....

....

....

2. What well-intentioned or not-so-well intentioned healing concepts came to your Sweetheart's direction from friends, family, and your church? What do some of their false notions tell you about your relationships and your own faith about healing?

....

....

....

3. In what ways have you seen momentary healing for your Sweetheart? How do you feel about God not healing your Love the way you or others hoped?

....

....

....

4. How has your view of God's choice of healing your spouse changed? What stayed the same? Has it strengthened your faith walk with God?

<u>Scripture for Reflection</u>

- James 5:14-16

....

....

....

....

- Exodus 23:25

....

....

....

....

- Psalm 6:2-3

....

....

....

....

- Psalm 73:26

....

....

....

....

- Revelation 21:4

....

....

....

....

Do you have any other thoughts on this chapter or Bible verses that come to mind?

....

....

....

Chapter SEVEN

Slammed Hard at the End

Paige stood radiant as she held her dad's arm when Mendelssohn's "Wedding March" started. Don walked her through the floral archway down the aisle to her groom and the officiant.

"Who gives this woman to be wed to this man?" the officiant asked.

"I do." Then Don sat down beside me after Paige took her husband-to-be's hand. I couldn't help but smile when I spotted a happy tear in the corner of Don's eye as the couple exchanged vows. I'd witnessed a miracle as God helped him experience another event on his five-year plan. Awestruck at God, I reveled in the moment of our daughter's marriage and the joy Don experienced that day.

After the ceremony, the photographer took portrait shots of family groups with the bride and groom. "Smile!" The camera's flash left us with floating spots in our vision, but photos from this time would become something we all would one day hold more dearly.

Don had been doing fairly well, not needing his cane or wheeled walker at our older daughter's wedding in December 2010. He only used a cane when he needed to walk or stand for long periods. He danced with her at the reception, twirling her around during the father-daughter dance. He also danced with me and our granddaughter, who was an infant at the time. As he participated in these weekend activities, several family members and guests were astonished at his energy level.

"Char, Don looks good," one of his brothers commented.

He still didn't look sick. Granted, he tired easily and required rest between events, but his heart was full. Don was definitely powered by love.

Down, But Not Out

Don leaned heavily on the lectern during Sunday services. Yet eventually, painful exhaustion forced him to preach from "the throne," an old, imposing wooden chair with a red velvet seat and back adorned with hand-carved embellishment. He could no longer walk through "the tunnel," a passageway with a small Sunday school space below the church linking it to the parsonage with steps leading down and then up. Teaching Sunday school sandwiched between two services wrung every ounce of energy from him. Instead, he rested on our sofa for an hour between services.

Toward the end of the service, he took prayer requests, relying on the pulpit to stand longer. His clear Lucite cane became a regular companion, but we purchased a wheeled walker for longer walks. Several congregation members expressed concern about his welfare, asking me, "Is Pastor Don alright? He looks tired."

"He's tired but good. He'd rather be here with all of you," I assured them as we shook hands in the greeting line after the service. Don sat on the walker's seat beside the large pump bottle of hand sanitizer. Smiling, he talked with attendees who stopped to shake his hand as they filed out of the sanctuary. We'd already begun praying for the right time for Don to step down as their pastor.

They had dealt with cancer in their own families before, so they recognized the eventuality of his death. Chemotherapy caused his blood platelets and white blood cells to plunge dangerously low, setting the stage for cancer's victory. His health degraded quickly over the preceding months.

***

However, May 2011 was a different story. Our youngest daughter married a couple of weeks after her college graduation. We attended her graduation with our family, which presented its own challenges for him, but we got through it. Walking that far took great effort. An older man on a golf cart shuttle stopped by as we headed across the college campus. "Would you like a ride? I can drop you off at the door." I could see the gentleman's concern for Don in his eyes.

"Sure. Why not?" Don replied. At first, he wanted to continue walking on his own but then relented. Setting his cane up against the seat, he grabbed the railing as I helped steady him onto it. As promised, the driver dropped us off right at the entrance door for the graduation ceremony. The effort to get him to see Rachel graduate was worth it. He beamed with pride as her name was called and she accepted her diploma. I couldn't help but bask in Don's joy and Rachel's accomplishment.

TRAINING FOR THE FIGHT

"Char, I want to walk Rachel down the aisle like I did for Paige at her wedding." He looked up at me from his chair at home, his eyes dull and filled with longing. His face had taken on a strange tanish complexion, indicating the early stages of liver failure, which we learned about later.

"I can ask one of my personal trainer friends to work with you if you'd like. He works with post-rehab clients. Do you want me to see what opening he's got on his schedule?"

"Yes, I'd like that." He smiled at me, looking hopeful for the big day.

Bill was willing and worked with Don's pain and fatigue for a couple of sessions, but unfortunately, he couldn't continue. "Char, he just can't do this. His pain is so bad. I'm afraid I'd be doing more harm than good," he told me in the personal trainers's office after Don's third session.

"Thank you, Bill. We appreciate your willingness to help him. It is what it is." I heaved a sigh.

Don's strength waned with each passing day due to the voracious growth of the cancer that threatened to put him in its chokehold. His pain levels were amplified by the tumor attached to the base of his spine. He tried doing the exercises so he could accomplish his goal, yet pain got the best of him.

***

We witnessed yet another incredible miracle on Rachel's wedding weekend. He was able to participate in the rehearsal and rehearsal dinner. Not only did he walk her down the church's aisle to give her to her groom, but he danced with her, our one-year-old granddaughter, and me. He loved every moment of our youngest daughter's special day. She relished this moment with him as well. He paid an exorbitant price to experience another important family event, but didn't care because he loved it all. Perhaps God used the failed training sessions to help us see His power at work in Don's final moments as he fulfilled his five-year plan.

WOLF PACK ATTACK

"When should I step down from the pulpit?" Don asked my opinion on this decision, which weighed heavily on our minds.

"I'll leave that up to you, but I imagine it should be soon."

"I'll wait until after Easter, I think. I don't want to put a damper on this important holiday.

Our church needs to focus on Jesus. I'll talk with the elders about it right afterward."

I could tell this was a hard decision for him to make. How horrible it must have been to realize so many last moments were rushing up fast.

Technically, he "retired" from the church in April but finished the Easter sermon series he had planned. The church council and regional director for our denomination forced him to let go of the pastorate, only for the director to step back into the church's pastorate that he'd filled before Don came to shepherd this congregation. Not one council member or the church council president-pastor relations chairman spoke with him about their concerns for him to quietly step down. It felt more like a corporate strategic move than church family business. Where was the Christian love and compassion?

Instead, the council president and regional director grilled and drilled Don in a special meeting as if he had committed some impropriety, even though he hadn't. It smacked of a wolf pack surrounding him, lunging for his throat. Several members of the church stood up and spoke in his defense.

Dave, the regional director, stated, "It has been brought to my attention that Pastor Don has not been fulfilling his pastoral duties for the majority of the time he's been here. Not only that, a survey conducted by the council a while ago conveyed deep dissatisfaction with his overall performance. We have no choice but to request that Pastor Don step down." He stood firm in his position.

The head elder stood up and spoke in Don's defense, "Pastor Don has taken an interest in our youth and Bible quiz team, which our previous pastors had not done. When notified, he visited members and their families in the hospital. He also conducted several funerals and weddings, never charging for his services. He's been actively involved with the Blessing of the Bikes for our chapter of Messiah Riders. When he's had chemotherapy infusions, he's ministered to several families whose loved ones were also going through infusions. He's been on death watches, met with several church attendees in counseling sessions, and averted potential disasters. His wife has ministered alongside him as often as she could while holding a job of her own and tending to his needs."

"He's the best pastor we've had in years!" a voice belted out from the crowded room. Certainly, that must have stung the regional director.

More church members spoke up, sharing all that Don had done for them and their family members, the support we had given to their children, and the times we stopped to chat with several church members even though we were running our errands or had frozen foods in our cart that were unintentionally defrosting. Yet, the regional director and council president stood proud, holding their ground. They gave him a severance package and retired him so he could receive his benefits. He never had a chance to step down gracefully on his own terms.

It certainly felt like a wolf pack attack.

I'd spent the time in our living room praying over this meeting and eavesdropping on some parking lot conversations behind the parsonage. Don relayed all of this to me afterward, as did the head elder and his wife when I spoke with her. Others conveyed their upset and disappointment over how the officials treated us, sharing their vantage point of that meeting. We felt such gratitude for their friendship and support. But the damage was done.

We sold many of our belongings to move from the parsonage into a townhouse apartment in a nearby city. It was much smaller than the parsonage, with two small bedrooms and a bathroom upstairs. His diminishing mobility made it impossible for him to travel up the stairs after moving in, even though he could when we had signed the lease just a few weeks prior. Since he had a colostomy, the bathroom was not an issue. He also had use of a bedside commode, and he slept on our sofa downstairs.

We made his bed on the couch every night, but he desperately needed a hospital bed. The home health nurse promptly ordered one, but our insurance didn't approve it for two months. The bed arrived a couple of days before his final hospital stay. However, they immediately approved a transport chair, which only worked in our home due to its small plastic wheels. So, I went to a thrift store, where I picked up a wheelchair with large rubber tires. I couldn't believe the ridiculous hoops we had to go through to secure what he desperately needed. Frustrated by insurance red tape, the nurse exclaimed, "He seriously needed them sooner. It's obvious!"

"I couldn't agree more," I said.

Body Slammed

Don had been the navigator for the two of us when we drove anywhere, while I could get lost in a paper bag. This time, the tables were turned. On our way to Pittsburgh from home, he argued with me about which direction to turn."Char, no! Take this exit," Don insisted, pointing with a wavering hand the direction he meant. His instructions would take us in the opposite direction of where we needed to go. I could tell his brain wasn't processing things correctly. So, I explained to him how I knew my course was correct. "Don, if we turn here, we'd end up in Latrobe. We have to take the turnpike to go to Pittsburgh."

He sat quietly, pondering the routes, and then, with embarrassment, mumbled, "You're right." At that point, he realized he couldn't trust his own navigation skills anymore. What a horrible, quiet ride.

We moved into our apartment in June. By July, his body filled up with fluid like a water balloon. Everything below his chest was so swollen with fluid that it looked as if his skin would burst open, adding to his misery. Home healthcare began making more frequent stops.

I hated leaving him alone during my workday, but I ensured he had food and drinks nearby so he wouldn't fall trying to get his lunch. I'd subscribed to cable television so he wouldn't get bored and time would pass quicker. Some friends would stop by to visit with him. I drove home for lunch when I could, but it wasn't always possible. I knew I had to keep my job to pay our bills, yet I felt pulled because he needed me. His friends were such a blessing. They helped take him to appointments when I couldn't and helped him with his lunch when they came to visit.

Don only made it upstairs once early on after we moved into our apartment. The physical therapist took him up so he could see what I had done with it. The only radiation treatments he had were during this short time. His doctor discovered a tumor on his coccyx that was pressing on his sciatic nerve during the time he led our former church. The oncologist, not having protocols to work from, ordered radiation treatments to shrink the tumor. These treatments scorched his backside so badly that he needed an ointment and gauze pads to make sitting somewhat bearable. Cancer treatments are so *barbaric!*

***

One evening at the end of July, I heard him rattle as he breathed. His home health nurse had warned us to watch for this ominous sign. Neither of us understood what caused it. When the nurse came for her scheduled appointment with him, we told her what we had heard. She listened with her stethoscope and then, wide-eyed, insisted that he needed immediate hospital treatment. However, Don had his oncology surgeon's appointment the next day, so he talked her into letting him wait. "Don't put it off any longer than that. You need medical attention now!" she pressed.

A friend from my work loaned Don a power scooter, a much-needed blessing. I took it apart in three manageable pieces and packed it in the trunk to take him to Pittsburgh.

As the clinic oncology nurse took his vitals, we told her about the sounds we heard and the visiting nurse's recommendation. "He certainly does have a rattle in his chest," she agreed. "I'll check with his oncology surgeon to get his input."

She stepped out for a moment to talk with the doctor. Suddenly, Don's colostomy bag burst open, filling the room with a putrid stench. I grabbed as many paper towels from the dispenser as possible to contain the brown, obnoxious goo. She came back while I helped him clean up. Her pallor waxed green, and she called the ostomy nurse to help change it. By now, the odor wafted down the hallway. It was good that the doctor arrived several minutes late, as we had it cleaned up by the time he arrived. When he listened to Don's lungs during the exam, he declared, "We are going to admit you to the hospital. This fluid must be drained."

The borrowed scooter helped so much as he rode it to the hospital wing from the medical offices connected by a series of halls and a skywalk. He couldn't have walked that far. I kept pace behind him along the way.

ICU nurses set him up with IVs and monitoring devices right away. While they were busy with him, I rode the scooter back to the parking garage, took it apart, and loaded it in the car to make it easier to go home late that night. I went back up to sit with him keeping him company and answer any questions the medical team needed. But around one o'clock in the morning, a nurse urged me to go home to rest. Our cell phones were our lifeline when I couldn't be there.

On my way home along the Pennsylvania Turnpike in the wee hours of the morning, my head bobbed as I fought to stay awake. One of the moments when I startled back awake, I saw part of the mountain rushing toward me on a curve. I quickly righted the car on the road. *Thank you, Lord, for waking me up. Please help me get home safely.* When I came home without Don, our orange kitty's warm greeting helped tame my anxiety. Morris looked for Don, seemingly confused by his absence. It was a very lonely, tense time for both of us.

Don's vitals had caused immediate concern; with his blood pressure so high, his head throbbed terribly. The medical staff rushed him into surgery. Unfortunately, the diuretic his doctor prescribed didn't relieve the fluid retention, which had caused his blood pressure to spike. A surgeon placed drain tubes between his ribs to release the pale amber fluid into a clear plastic container with measurement markings on the front. After surgery, Don remained in the intensive care unit (ICU). I was an emotional mess as he flowed in and out of consciousness.

In the meantime, my cell phone contract expired, so I had to change phone plans at that critical time. A friend took me to the phone store near the hospital. I needed to maintain an open line of communication with Don and his medical team as much as possible. Thankfully, she had clarity of thought because I definitely did not. I slept with my phone when I had to go home since I couldn't stay in ICU with him overnight. One of Don's nurses also charged his phone with her personal phone charger. It was our lifeline that connected us.

DOWN FOR THE COUNT

Don's medical team recommended calling the family in to say goodbye to him before he passed away. His situation looked bleak. I felt so numb I could hardly think straight. My hands trembled as I tried to target each key to dial my kids' phone numbers. Then, hesitantly, I told each one what we expected. They drove several hours, coming as quickly as possible to spend time with their dad before he was gone.

The attending physician found a clot in Don's jugular vein a day or two later, and a staff surgeon implanted a mesh filter to prevent the clot from reaching his heart. This event prompted him to write his advance directive, clearly indicating, "Do Not Resuscitate." He seemed to accept the inevitable, looking up at me as he laid the pen on his tray. The twinkle in his eye—a trait I loved—was gone.

He said in a raspy, whispered tone, "Char, I can't keep doing this for you and the kids. No more surgery. No heroic acts to save me. I am ready to go when the Lord wants me." His empty, dull eyes told me he knew he would die soon. At that moment, I had to accept this reality too.

Tears poured down my cheeks, "It's okay for you to go Home. God will take care of me. I don't want you to go, but I understand the time is near."

Another challenge hit me when my phone rang with frightening news. Our son-in-law told us that our youngest daughter was hospitalized as well, several hours away. Her blood sugar and ketones were dangerously high. She was diagnosed with type 1 diabetes. I felt so very torn—again. This was the second time I felt caught between a rock and a hard place for her and Don. She needed me, but he needed me. He wasn't always able to answer questions for the medical team. I needed to do that for him while Rachel's husband stayed beside her. I also couldn't handle driving that far on my own either. So, I kept in contact with her through my son-in-law and other family members who provided support for them. I wished I could split myself in two. Thankfully, God placed her in excellent care.

After his tubes and wires were removed except for a basic IV, Don's mom, brother, sister-in-law, and sister came to visit, which calmed his anxiety. Their visit was well-timed. But then, after they left, he needed something from me too.

"Char, I need a hug so badly." Before, it was too hazardous with all the IVs, drain tubes, and monitor wires. Now that he was free, I could hug him. "Can you come up here with me?"

"There's not enough room for me on either side."

He pressed the nurse call button and asked them to shift him to one side of the bed. After they had done so, I lay down beside him and cuddled. The unsettling scent of death lingered. I shut it out as we melted in each other's arms.

"Char, I want you to know that it's okay for you to marry again when you are ready. Please, don't pine away for me. You've got a lot of life left to live after I'm gone." I couldn't help but cry. Only a couple of days later, he went to hospice. I had no choice but to accept the reality of Don's impending death.

THOUGHTS ON THIS CHAPTER

Accepting the end of life is hard. It jolts you to your innermost being when you realize your spouse is leaving soon. Denial tactics no longer work, and the tough stuff has to be done. How easy it is to fall apart. Sometimes, Satan and his cronies kick us and our Sweethearts when we are down. Yet God, in His infinite wisdom and foreknowledge, is not shocked. He knows it all, giving us glimpses of Himself and His work in our crushing situations. We must trust in His love and goodness at such a time as this.

FOR REFLECTION

The stages I experienced knowing Don was dying were:

- » Shock, numbness—I felt so numb I could hardly think clearly.
- » Resignation—My hands trembled as I tried to target each key to dial my kids' phone numbers to let them know their dad would die soon.
- » Distraught—I was an emotional mess as he flowed in and out of consciousness.
- » Acceptance—Don knew he would die soon and so did I. At that moment, I had to accept this reality too.
- » Clinginess—I slept with my phone when I had to go home since it was our lifeline that connected us.
- » Overwhelmed—I felt very torn again to be with Don and Rachel.

Questions for Reflection

1. If you've already lost your Sweetheart or are about to, how did (do) you feel? What were (are) the thoughts racing through your head?

_____

_____

_____

_____

2. How did friends and family support you during your Sweetheart's last few days or weeks?

_____

_____

3. What final precious moments did you experience with your Love?

_____

_____

4. What blessings do you see in hindsight?

_____

_____

Scripture for Reflection

- Philippians 2:1-4,17

_____

_____

- Philippians 3:20-21

_____

_____

- 2 Timothy 4:6-8

- Psalm 91:1-12

Do you have any other Bible passages or thoughts about this time in your life?

Chapter EIGHT

Rising from the Ashes

Silence. The stillness disturbed me. I sat up on the edge of the hide-a-bed sofa in Don's hospice room as the lights from the reflective garden shone through the curtains. Something had awakened me around 5:30 am. It was so eerily quiet that I suspected something was amiss. I padded barefoot to his bedside to check on him. He lay strangely still, so I touched his hand. Cold. His face looked more relaxed and peaceful than I'd seen in a long time. His mouth and eyelid pulled down on one side, reminders of the Bell's palsy he'd controlled well since his teen years. He was gone.

Gut-wrenched sobbing overtook me as I grasped that the inevitable had happened while I slept. Guilt pangs stung as I realized I'd missed his passing. *I should have sat with him through it. They told me it could take a couple of days. Who knew? I was so exhausted it was impossible for me to stay awake. What's wrong with me?*

I called the nurse. She came in and checked his vitals. With a faint smile, she told me, "I believe he's gone. I will get the doctor to confirm. I'm sorry for your loss." *How could she handle doing her job, knowing that every patient she cared for would die?*

The doctor confirmed his passing. "Time of death, 4:20 am."

The night before, my friend MaryAnn and Don's friend had been in this room with us. Don, incoherent, wasn't even aware of their presence, I'm sure. We chatted for a while, and then they both went to the chapel to pray for Don's home-going and for me. After quite some time, they came back to the room and hugged me. "Call me if you need anything," MaryAnn had said. Then they left.

Now I felt a nudge from the Lord to text MaryAnn: "He's gone."

"What time did he pass?" she asked.

"Sometime between 4:30 or 5:00 this morning, I think. He was gone when I checked on him around 5:30."

"Interesting. I dreamed around that same time that he and I were walking and talking together when we came to some beautiful white stairs that led upward into the clouds, but I couldn't go up. I heard the most beautiful singing. He went up the stairs, singing with the voices above, his voice blending in perfectly with theirs. He disappeared into those clouds. Then I woke up." She had escorted Don to Heaven's stairs as I slept.

***

"I'll leave you time to spend with your husband, Mrs. Engelhardt. Take as much time as you need." The nurse's compassion helped soften the emotional blow. I sat with him for quite a while, thanking God for our life together and confessing every wrong thing I believed I'd ever done that hurt Don.

Afterward, I stepped out to let the nurse know I'd said my goodbyes. She asked me to wait out in the hall while the doctor prepared him for transport. After what seemed an eternity, ambulance workers wheeled a gurney into his room. They soon emerged with Don, covered head to toe in a white sheet, pushing it out a side door and securing it in an ambulance. I felt like an invisible hand ripped my heart out of my chest. It seemed as though I'd died too. I didn't want to be there any longer. So, I put my belongings into my overnight bag and headed out to my car.

What Now?

Ugh. You've got to be kidding! Of all things, a flat tire, I groaned. Standing beside my car in the hospice center's parking lot for a moment, I thought through my options and called my friend to help me get the tire fixed or replaced. *Praise the Lord! A tire store isn't far from here.* So, I left the hospice center, bumping along to a tire shop with MaryAnn following me.

It felt like Satan face-planted me in the ashes of my grief, amplifying my aloneness. A couple of hundred dollars that I didn't have later, I motored home in my grief bubble. As I maneuvered through traffic in a haze, I mulled over a conversation Don had with the hospice chaplain the day he arrived at the center and had been coherent for a brief time. This chaplain had pastored a church in the next town, so he was familiar with the challenges we faced in our final church. He'd witnessed how the last few pastors and their families had been mistreated. He confirmed what we'd endured but that our ministry to that congregation was not in vain. God knew we needed peace, especially for Don, and that the regional stronghold we had faced was indeed real.

"When it rains, it pours" is an adage that rings true. It was certainly raining in my stormy little bubble. *I could use Your umbrella, God,* I whined. *Will the rest of my life alone will be like this?*

A familiar song started playing on the radio that I had heard several times before traveling back and forth to Pittsburgh while Don was in the hospital—"Beautiful Things" by Gungor. The lyrics spoke to how I felt in my heart. *How will I be able to go through life without Don, my anchor in life? I hurt so much from losing my high school sweetheart. Will I ever find life again?* I had no idea how God would bring good out of this mess.

That evening, as I stared into the distance with my thoughts, I could see the hills silhouetted against the night sky, with houses dotting them, revealed by their lights. I felt very lost. Wounded. Alone. The notion of how God could make me new seemed impossible. I played my anthem song as I looked through photographs and watched some videos I found of Don preaching. Tears showered away some of my anguish, at least for the moment.

I felt like half a person going through my days. Some moments felt as if a storm cloud hovered over my head, gushing raindrops. Others seemed like I was trying to tread water, barely able to keep my head above it. *How could I possibly go through life like this?* I still lived and worked in Pennsylvania, while my kids and their families lived in Ohio. None of my family lived near me. I put on my professional face at work but left my grief at home. Privately, I reflected on Don through pictures and music that we enjoyed together through the years. *Will my memories disappear?* I worried. It scared me, which made no sense at all. *How will I go on without him, Lord? Did I do something wrong that you would take him away? Or did You reward him early?* I desperately wanted to know. So, I prayed often for God's answers.

DEATH CLEANSING

When I opened the door to my apartment after the funeral, Don's medical equipment and supplies stared me in the face. They made our home—my home—repulsive. I was so disgusted that I decided they had to go now. Angry, ugly-crying, I hurled the opened tape and bandage packages into the trash. These reminders of his terrible suffering were more than I could bear.

My first task was to call the medical supply company. "Hello? I need the hospital bed and transport chair picked up. Unfortunately, my husband passed away."

"We are sorry for your loss," the customer service representative from the medical supply store responded. "We can send someone out tomorrow around two pm."

"Thank you. That works." I choked back tears.

Next, I called the hospice center. "I have several unopened boxes of bandages, tape, and other supplies here. Could you use any of them?" We had received a fresh shipment of them just a few days before Don went to the hospital. *What a waste! If they can use them, I'd feel better about it.*

"Yes, ma'am. We certainly can. Thank you so much." I couldn't handle going there again myself. It was too painful. A friend was willing to pick them up and donate them for me since she lived not far from there. I thanked God for her friendship and willingness to sit with me in my grief. What would I do without Christian friends? It was a relief to have those visible reminders of cancer's brutality out of my home.

NAVIGATING SOLO

Learning to manage challenges alone after Don's death was hard. My house and car keys waved at me from the backseat of my locked car after work one afternoon. *What now? I wish Don were here to help me, but I can't ask him.* Suddenly, I remembered that AAA member information had come in the mail. *A locksmith!* They will send out a locksmith! Giddy with this news, I called them on my cell phone, and indeed they would. The man who came out showed sympathy for my plight. He skillfully tripped the car lock. Voila! Twenty-five dollars got me out of my jam.

"Thank you!"

"No problem, ma'am. Sorry for your loss." There it was again. *Sigh.*

I missed Don's incredible ability to problem-solve. We'd been a team. *Can you have a team of one? Not as far as I know.* So I began asking myself in sticky situations, *What would Don say or do?*

***

Decision-making was difficult when I needed input. Family and friends became my sounding boards and sources of wise counsel on finances, car problems, and more. Sometimes, I found it difficult to trust my own judgment. *What if I make a huge, costly mistake?* I feared.

Red tape for insurance and final bills still awaited me to cut through it, demanding so much time and energy. I shuffled bills, claim forms, and letters around on my dining table, feeling overwhelmed. When Don died, our finances were in a serious deficit, even though, at one point, God miraculously canceled some of his medical debt. *What would it have been like if that debt had remained?* I shuddered to think. Scarcely able to live on my paycheck until the insurance came through, I called my landlord and the utility companies. "My husband passed away this week, and I'm waiting for his life insurance to come through. Can you give me two or three more weeks? I should receive it by then." Hesitated silence followed.

Finally, a voice on the other end of the call spoke up, "Yes, ma'am. We will note that on your account. If anything changes, please contact us immediately. Sorry for your loss." *My loss?* The way that sounded made me cringe. *I haven't misplaced him. Oh, well. They're trying to be kind. At least I have an extension for my payment due date.*

It was annoyingly interesting that a small life insurance policy his mother took out when he was a child was the worst group to process a claim. This policy took longer for me to get released due to the extensive documentation they required. On the other hand, our primary life insurance policy, worth far more, took the least time with fewer requirements.

Digging Out

I pulled out a notepad and carefully figured out I needed to separate my money into different accounts: one for short-term expenses, one to fill in gaps until I could build up my client base at work, and another for retirement. I also replaced my ailing car, which had racked up hundreds of dollars in repairs with no end in sight. I did my best to make this money last *and* work for me. Don's foresight in taking out a life insurance policy to help me get on my feet if—when he died was such a Godsend.

My health insurance's first premium bill, which I paid on my own, stunned me. *"How much?"* my voice cracked. "This is just for me. How can my premium be so close to what it cost for both of us while my husband was being treated for cancer?" Dollar signs sprouted wings and flew out the proverbial window. Those payments took a ginormous, unexpected chunk of my funds, so I looked for other insurance to cover my medical expenses.

God Reaches Down to Me

I decided to attend the church that welcomed us after we left the last church Don pastored. Sitting alone seemed awkward, yet I did it before he died when he was on the pulpit. Here, another pastor stood on this church's platform. I sat isolating myself in my protective bubble from the other people in the auditorium.

In the mid-week Bible study, the focus on forgiveness tugged on my heart as if the Holy Spirit wanted to crack open its door to clear out all my prickly grudges and pain. *How can I forgive our former church leadership for what they did to us while Don was so ill and still effectively leading the congregation? I need to, Lord, but I don't want to!* My inner turmoil interrupted the pastor's discussion questions. This topic was just what our Great Physician ordered.

I still emotionally gushed blood from the wounds inflicted by narcissistic leaders. Even though I had taught about forgiveness numerous times before, it was my turn to be the student.

Focused on my healing, I began to experience freedom. God kept knocking on my heart's door until I finally accepted my responsibility to let go, allowing Him to haul those grudges away.

BREACH OF SECURITY

Grudges certainly weren't my only turmoil. At night, anxiety over personal safety kept me awake until one or two o'clock in the morning. How silly it seemed because Don couldn't protect me before. Just his presence in the house at night gave me comfort though. So, I bought a burglar bar for the front door since my landlord didn't believe it necessary to install a deadbolt on the doors of these townhouse apartments. I usually wedged it under the door handle on my way to bed.

After work one evening, I relaxed on my sofa, watching television with Morris curled up beside me. The front door handle suddenly rattled. I froze. Someone was messing with it. With ninja stealth, I got up from the couch, crept up to the door, and grabbed the burglar bar, holding it like a baseball bat. I yelled, "What do you want?"

Listening intently, I stood poised to bash the intruder in the head. The self-defense instructor in me stood ready for battle. Nothing. *What should I do?* Barely able to breathe from my heart pounding so hard, I decided to call the police. I kept watch on the door with the bar at my ready while I waited for the police to show up.

When they arrived, the amused officers laughed. "No one's ever had a problem in this neighborhood! But," they assured me in a sympathetic tone, "we'll check it out." About an hour later, the police came back. "Your next-door neighbor's best man, who was intoxicated, got the wrong door. He was confused when you yelled because he heard you instead of his friend." Their kind understanding calmed my heart.

Sheepish yet relieved, I thanked the officers. Then I closed and locked the door behind them, wedging the burglar bar firmly under the door handle.

The couple next door came over the following day to apologize for the scare they believed they had caused. He and his wife offered to help watch out for me since they discovered Don had died—young newlyweds watching out for a midlife widow. I appreciated that all was well and God provided extra eyes and ears watching out for my safety. I was also thrilled I didn't have to clobber my neighbor's best man.

I can't say I felt as though life could turn around. I identified with Job in the Bible, an emotional wreck in my ash heap of loss. Although life had turned upside down, I hung on to hope that God would make me new. He could make beautiful things out of my ashes. Don had been such a stabilizer for me because he had grown up in a healthy family with a strong sense of direction. He was also an extrovert, whereas I was an introvert. *We* ended, and *I* began. It was time to get to know who I was, what I thought, and even what I wanted in life apart from him. So, I asked God to help me craft a plan for moving on.

LIFE BEGINS

I disliked being stuck in Pennsylvania, working at the gym, and going home to an empty apartment. So, I sent my resume out to gyms in North Central Ohio so I could live closer to my adult kids. Finally, after a long, frustrating search, a gym near Akron hired me. I also found an affordable townhouse apartment near my new job that would accept Morris. My son's family and my two daughters' families were all within an hour's drive from me. I hired an inexpensive moving company to move me and my belongings four hours back home, put Morris in his pet carrier, and didn't look back. *Goodbye, Pennsylvania!*

This move was my fresh start. I decorated my new apartment on a tight budget with colors and styles I liked, finding treasures at closeout and thrift stores. I needed my own style. Also, I loved my son's dynamic, contemporary church, which had doctrine that aligned with mine. Being a regular Christian in the church pew felt good where I could blend in. God began pulling things together for me. Without such a long drive, I could spend time with my kids and their families. I didn't feel so alone anymore.

***

Riding my bike on bike trails was also on my list. I picked up a bike and a bike rack on sale at a local discount store but felt awkward getting back into riding again. It had been *years*. The Cuyahoga Valley parks boasted beautiful trails, so I set out little by little. Although I was wobbly at first, it wasn't long before I rode several miles on my own. Don had not been good with following through on physical activities like this one. Cycling was totally mine.

Gradually, I began to see the lyrics of my anthem song unfold: hope—my life in Christ as His child. New life grew slowly even though grief often poked its nose in my life. God did indeed have a plan for my future apart from Don. He wasn't punishing me for some unknown sin. I realized He took Don Home as an early reward. I didn't like it, but I couldn't change it either. All I could do was change my direction in life. God had plans for me. Even though I could make my plans, God would order my steps.[13]I needed to trust Him to lead me into my new life.

13   Proverbs 16:9

THOUGHTS ON THIS CHAPTER

When you suddenly find yourself alone as *me* or *I*, but you were used to *we* and *us*, nothing can be more disorienting in life. Suddenly, part of you is gone, but in reality, your Sweetheart is gone. Eventually, you rediscover yourself.

You may be tempted to enshrine your Love by keeping their things just as they left them. However, we must move on eventually because refusing to accept that your Love died is unhealthy. This delusion has been known to cause some widows and widowers to become mentally and spiritually unwell. Eventually, you figure it out, but please know that God has a wonderful plan for your life. This place isn't our home, but someday we will go Home too. What a sweet reunion it will be!

FOR REFLECTION

Here are some of the elements of grief I experienced at this stage:

» False guilt—I felt overwhelming guilt for not being awake with Don as he passed away, yet I knew I couldn't stay awake from exhaustion.
» Feeling disoriented—I felt so very alone, almost like half a person walking through life in a daze.
» Repulsed by medical equipment, places, or procedures—The presence of Don's medical supplies disgusted me so much that I decided they had to go. These things reminded me of the terrible suffering Don endured.
» Difficulty making decisions alone—Sometimes I found it difficult to trust my own judgment. I was afraid of making a costly mistake.
» Greater need for a support network and company—With my cat as my companion, I decided to move closer to my kids after my lease was up.

» Rediscovering self—This was my fresh start. I decorated my apartment on a tight budget with colors and styles I liked from closeout stores. I needed to find my own style. It was time to get to know who *I* was, what *I* thought, and even what *I* wanted in life apart from him.

Questions for Reflection

1. What mental cameo moment replays in your mind from when your Sweetheart died? How do those memories make you feel?

....

....

2. What regrets still haunt you now?

....

....

3. How did God show up for you during and after your Love's passing?

....

....

4. What financial stresses and hurdles did you face? How did you get them under control? How did God provide for your needs?

....

....

5. What decisions are difficult for you to make without your Sweetheart? Who can you ask for help?

....

....

....

6. What action plan do you have for your life right now? If you don't have one, prayerfully consider working out a plan for the next five years. Where do you envision yourself, both personally and professionally? What things would you like to do or see?

....

....

....

7. What changes would you make in your life as you allow the Holy Spirit to search your heart and guide your pen?

....

....

....

Scripture for Reflection

- Isaiah 43:19

....

....

....

- 2 Kings 2:11-14

....

....

....

- Proverbs 16:9

....

....

....

Any other thoughts or Bible passages that come to mind?

....

....

....

Chapter NINE

Finding Love Again

Instant messages popped up in front of me like dandelions in the yard. "Hey, baby! You're hot! Let's chat." "I'm a Virgo. What's your sign?" "God told me you're the woman for me!"

Messages like these, and some that I would never repeat, littered my computer screen. Ugh! Disgusting. Click, click, click. I shot down instant message balloons like space aliens in a video game. The world of Internet dating was an overwhelming, scary scene, educating me about the ploys of predators. I hadn't completed my profile yet; it had only a couple of photos of myself and basic information like my age, widowed, height, weight, and hair color. That's all it took for the wolf pack to gang up on me. I immediately shut down the instant messaging feature, only accepting inbox messages, which are traceable. *That should reduce the number of casanovas—I hope.*

Almost a year had passed while loneliness still overwhelmed me. I loved having my kids and grandkids around, but an emptiness still echoed in my heart, one they couldn't fill. So after wondering how to begin dating again, I joined a couple of online dating sites because some friends had found their husbands on some of them. At least, people on dating sites are looking for other single people who are looking for someone, too. Since I was looking for God's man for me, I needed to find reasonable Christian men looking for a reasonable Christian woman for a potential wife.

It took me several tries to write my bio. *Who am I? What do I want from life now? What qualities do I want in a potential husband?* These questions simmered in my mind, prompting me to put my five-year goals out there. I even had photos taken for a few reasons, this being one of them. Then, all of a sudden, I got more reasonable interest. A wink, a smile, and even a few conversations began.

"What happened to your husband?"

"What are you looking for in a potential husband?"

"How long have you been widowed?"

"What's your ideal date?"

These were all good questions that caused me to pursue knowing more about myself to find the right man to love. What a learning process!

MEAT MARKET

"Hey, what do you say we find a quiet, out-of-the-way place together?" a male gym member asked. He had corralled me with his hands across the office doorway leading out onto the gym floor. His breath reeked of alcohol, and he had a reputation as a womanizer. I wanted nothing to do with him, so I quickly ducked under his arm, prepared to defend if needed.

"I've got an appointment coming up." I made myself scarce by heading to the front desk near the entrance, where lots of people were checking in. I gave up looking at the men around me at the health club and church. It was so difficult to know who was taken and who was not, and whether or not they were safe. *What a meat market*, I thought.

Yet, internet dating certainly isn't for everyone. Mostly, these dating sites seemed to be a meat market, too, often for disgruntled divorced people. It also seemed like a place for never-married men to set up a personal photo gallery dedicated to their manhood, displaying photos of them posed with their dog, boat, motorcycle, or hot car. *Oh, Puh-lease! There have got to be some reasonable, mentally stable, emotionally secure-in-their-masculinity kind of guys.* Sigh. *At least I knew everyone on these is looking for someone. Where are the level-headed Christian men looking for a sensible Christian woman to marry?* I sat on my sofa staring at my laptop with Morris purring over my shoulder. Dating in midlife became frustrating.

After a few disheartening dates, I considered giving up. A couple of men I dated for a while were nothing like what they claimed to be in their profiles. Some drank and smoked, several worshiped at St. Mattress, and others thought premarital sex was okay. *What happened to biblical Christian values?*

One Christian man who lived within the local community met me for dinner at a mid-level restaurant. An air of superiority hovered over him during our conversation. It seemed that he thought I was "beneath" him. *I need to keep looking,* I told myself.

What he said sealed it. "I think I should tell you," he began in a guarded tone, "I had an affair on my wife, so she divorced me. Is it even appropriate for me to consider marrying again?"

Rather than giving him my blunt, pat answer, "God bless you in your search," I explained how he could prayerfully look through Scripture to learn what God would say about his question. I thanked him for the lovely meal and conversation, wished him well, and left.

Several Christian men had serious issues. One turned out to be a scary online encounter. We had several conversations using the messaging feature on the website. Some of his information didn't make sense, but we decided that a real-time phone discussion might clarify things. So we agreed to call each other. *Click-click. Click-click,* I heard when I answered his call. *Hmm. Bad connection?* I tried calling him. *Click-click. Click-click.* Suddenly, I had a frightening light-bulb moment. *He's trying to call me from prison!* My self-defense alert system was blaring code red. *Abandon the conversation! Report it!* Immediately, I blocked him online and then contacted the administrator of the Christian dating site.

Sure enough, he wasn't who he claimed to be. All his profile photos of him in jeans and a white t-shirt vanished from the website. *Whew!* Relieved, I didn't want anyone else to encounter him. They might make a trip to see him that would have an unfortunate ending. Wouldn't you know, he reappeared a few days later under a different profile name and different photos in a white t-shirt and jeans. Again, I reported him. Unsafe people are very deceptive. I saw it as confirmation of God warning me about him.

Disheartened, I stayed offline for a while. *Lord, why did you take Don away from me? If he were still here, I wouldn't be dealing with the whole adult dating mess. What did I do wrong?* I was heartbroken, and loneliness flooded over me.

TRY, TRY AGAIN

I wanted to find God's Christian man for me, but it seemed like looking for a needle in a haystack. After a couple of weeks' hiatus, I cautiously tried again. One evening after work, I sat down on my sofa as Morris purred in my ear behind me. Profile matches had piled up, and I filed through matches and messages. This one looked intriguing, yet intimidating: "If your profile's true, WE'VE GOT TO MEET!!!!"

Stunned, I sat in silence, staring at my computer screen. *Do I chat with him or not? There is safety in distance.* So, while Mr. Ambitious chatted with me, another man had also begun messaging me. Mr. Ambitious lived about a five-hour drive north of me. *Ugh! That's too far away. I couldn't afford to drive to see him regularly.* The other guy lived in my area. But after three dates with Mr. Local, I decided he had too many red flags for my comfort. *Too bad, though.* He lived closer, was part of the worship team at his church, and liked to work out and cycle on the local trails. *Nope. Not a good match.*

I could barely earn a living wage, so I couldn't see how Mr. Ambitious and I could manage the distance for very long. I must admit, though, he was intriguing—a bit of an interesting nut, and sweet. Dismayed, I told him, "You know, long-distance relationships usually fail. You live too far away."

He seemed to have a solution for everything, though. "I've got a plane. I can fly to see you!"

"What? You have a plane?" Astonished, I leaned back in my seat. *Was he telling the truth or lying to impress me?*

"Yes. If I understand roughly where you live, there is a university airport not far from you," he reasoned. Mr. Ambitious was right.

Hmm. If he can fly down, that would be reasonable. We continued messaging, texting, and eventually talking on the phone for a few months before actually meeting face-to-face.

"Don't you think we should go live with this relationship?" he asked.

I cautiously agreed.

He was indeed a pilot, but he didn't have a plane in flyable condition. He owned a couple of airplane kits to build, which wouldn't take him anywhere anytime soon. He'd been looking for a used aircraft to purchase, so dating gave him a greater incentive to get one sooner rather than later to close the distance between us. Since he made a tremendous effort to secure a plane, he won some of my approval.

Meeting for the First Time

Mr. Ambitious, whose name was Boaz, had to drive to meet me for the first few times since he didn't have a flyable plane yet. Sitting down on the stylish sofa in the hotel lobby to meet him for our dinner date, I checked his photo on my phone so I knew who I was looking for. As I looked up, a gentleman emerged from the hall. *It looks like him, but he seems a bit professorly. We'll see how this goes.* I pondered my exit strategy in case this was another dud date.

As I stood up, he looked my way. "Hello, Boaz?" I waited as he stood there, scanning me. He seemed politely cautious, wearing his work shirt with the company logo. *Well, he must work for the business he claims to, or he has an elaborate scheme to get me to believe he does what he says.* I had let my adult kids know about my date so that if anything went wrong, they knew where I was and who I would meet. I discovered that he was an engineering manager leading an advanced engineering group in the automotive industry in the Detroit metroplex. *No wonder he could afford to buy a plane and fly!*

"Yes, and you must be Charlaine?" He smiled. "Nice to finally see you face-to-face." Boaz ushered me out the door, offering to drive us to the restaurant, but I opted to meet him there in case he was some crazed lunatic.

Boaz was a gentleman who held the door for me and pulled the chair out at our dining table. His reservedness made me think this might be our only date. *Oh, well. If that's what happens, no worries.*

Dinner felt like a job interview, as most first in-person dates do. Even though we had discussed a lot of the usual things adult Christian singles want to know, questions and answers flowed back and forth. As we talked during our meal, he revealed that he had been divorced. *Hmmm. Why? What happened? Who did what to whom? Abuse? Neglect? Affair?* He revealed that his ex-wife had several affairs and was likely a mismatch in the first place. I shared more details about my late husband's cancer and death than in our previous discussions, as well as our ministry together. And then, I noticed a twinkle in his eye. He began to look at ease. I wasn't yet.

I also wanted to know how badly he was affected by adult ADD. I could see its effects, but no red flags stood out.

"You told me you'd like to tour Stan Hywet Hall and Gardens in Akron. According to its website, it looks like a nice place to explore. Can I pick you up tomorrow morning around ten?" he asked, not realizing my safety antennas were on high alert. I didn't want him to know where I lived yet.

"I can meet you at your hotel and drive together," I offered.

"Great! I'll see you then." His face lit up.

Is he glad I didn't send him back home? Maybe, I thought. *But then again, he could be intrigued with me. Who knows?*

He mentioned during our drive that he expected someone taller. I'm not sure what he expected. After all, my profile stated I was only five-foot-one and one hundred and twenty pounds. He also knew I was a personal trainer working in a gym. Evidently, I wasn't quite what he anticipated. He stood five-foot-nine, relatively short for a man, so what I saw in front of me was exactly what I read on his profile. He claimed to be a runner, which I found out later that he did indeed run. *So far, so good. No surprises!*

A Fairytale Moment

The following morning, we took his rental car to the Goodyear mogul's beautiful historic home and gardens, which intrigued us both. He paid for my ticket with his. I was prepared to pay, just in case. "Thank you," I accepted the ticket and followed him to the guide's station. As we explored the grand mansion, I noticed he knew a lot about the impressive architecture and furnishings. I'd always been fascinated with historic homes but felt out of my league because of his remarkable knowledge of certain types of architecture and furnishings.

Afterward, the garden path beckoned us. I wasn't sure what to do as he reached over and confidently took my hand. *Am I even in-like?* I wondered. *It's way too early to know.*

I gently clasped his hand anyway when he reached out to me. We strolled through the meticulously cultivated shrubs and blooms. The scent of roses and lilacs swirled around us. We talked, smiled, and laughed as we admired the impressive veranda of the Tudor Revival, then circled beyond to a neatly patterned brick path tucked away beneath lush foliage. He stopped, gently swung me around toward him, and kissed me. *Wow! What do I do with this? Is this the first date or the second?* His warm lips were tender, and his embrace gentle. It was nice, but thoughts danced in my head. *Should I have kissed him back or objected? Am I cheating on Don? No. Remember, Don died, and it's "until death do us part." But am I ready?* My brain floundered in confusion as much as my heart. We nervously giggled and blushed on the "Kissing Lane," as we affectionately named it later.

I pondered our first meeting as we exchanged goodbyes after lunch on Sunday. *He went to church with me this morning! He knew the songs and had no problem looking up the Bible passages. None of my other dates did. I'm kind of in-like,* I mused. Then, smiling to myself, I drove back to my apartment.

FALLING FOR LOVE

Boaz promised he would purchase a plane to fly down to see me, which he did about three months later into our dating time. His divorce had happened around the same time my widowhood started, and we met each other about a year afterward. We were both healing and growing, but were we "in like" yet? I discovered later that he proceeded into our relationship with a guarded heart while fascinated with me, yet fearing I would break it. I felt wary, but not in the same way as he was. Mine came from the ouches from horrible dates.

Since he needed to find a plane to fly to see me, he asked me to go along with him to check one out. A road trip to southern Ohio to look at an airplane truly changed my heart. We talked about some of his plane searches while driving along the interstate. So many sellers tried to hide or leave out serious problems.

Hmmm. Sounds almost like dating!

He told me that when he went to check them out, he was sorely disappointed. "I hope this plane is exactly what Harry says it is. He said he hates getting rid of it but can no longer fly. He's in his nineties, impaired by his health." He glanced over at me every once in a while, then back to the road. I wondered what gearwheels were churning in his head.

Turning onto a side road toward a tiny airport south of Columbus, Ohio, we kept our eyes open for road signs. "I hope it is too. Maybe this man is a Christian praying for the right pilot to love his "baby" plane." I hoped Boaz could tell whether God's hand was in it. Skepticism was written on his face.

"We'll see," he stated matter-of-factly. Eventually, we pulled up to a somewhat rundown airport building with a rusty mechanics hangar beside it. Outside sat an old, rickety wooden picnic bench, and a tree with a well-worn tire swing hung from a large branch. A small red plane from the 1960s waited on the runway for its prospective owner to test-fly it. After parking at the back of the airport office, we strolled around to the front, then headed inside. The office smelled like a blend of mustiness with aviation fuel. It was decorated with various metal flight signs and old photographs of local pilots from a bygone era. It had a worn antique oak desk with a tattered office chair in which a senior man sat.

"Boaz Martin?" he said.

"Yes! Harry? Nice to meet you." With a gentle smile, he reached out to shake the gentleman's trembling hand.

"Likewise. Well, let's go out. I'll show you the plane and then take you up in it," Harry proudly announced. As he stood up, he was head and shoulders taller than Boaz. The two looked like a dad and son walking together, heading over to the vintage aircraft. They stepped up onto a safety tread on the wing, sat down in the pilot and co-pilot seats, and then began checking out the instrument panel. The plane had been well cared for but definitely needed updates.

Boaz looked at me with concern, fastened his seatbelt, and placed the headset on his ears while Harry closed the cockpit. His look worried me.

After all the necessary pre-flight checks, Harry bellowed, "Clear!" and started the plane. It hummed. They took off on the runway, and the sporty red plane deftly climbed out of sight.

I sat down on the picnic bench to wait, carefully checking to ensure no bird droppings would smear on my light gray shorts. The sun warmed my shoulders as I watched them disappear from view.

After a long while, I heard them approaching the runway and watched them land. Boaz's eyes were huge as he climbed out of the plane. I wondered about that look but waited to ask later.

Then Boaz came over to me and offered an unsolicited answer to my inner question. "I saw my life flash before my eyes! Harry's hand tremors are really *bad*. He wanted to take off on the short runway, but I talked him into using the longer one. Unfortunately, the heat today makes takeoff distances longer to get airborne. Oh, my. Thank you, Jesus!" he exclaimed.

Shocked at what I heard, I decided I should have prayed more, but then again, I did pray, and God brought them safely back. Harry wanted us to follow him into his hangar because he had some supplies that went with the plane. Boaz kindly listened to him as they rummaged together through a green wooden trunk. I stood leaning against the doorway, watching them. I could tell this man was selling his "baby," which he pampered. My heart melted at the tremendous respect Boaz showed Harry, reassuring him that he would indeed take good care of it. I saw Christ's love in action, which meant the world to me. My heart melted.

"Now, you remind him, just pull out the choke this much." Harry showed me as he measured from the tip of his index finger to his first knuckle while we walked back to the airport office.

"Okay, I will," I assured him. We waved goodbye, then drove away.

We returned a couple of weeks later to pick up the plane, and so Boaz could pay Harry for it. I could see a tear in the elderly man's eye. His wife had died between the time Boaz checked out the plane and when we returned for it. This sweet brother in Christ lost his wife *and* his plane in a very short time. God confirmed that my love wasn't misplaced because of Boaz's compassion for this man's loss of his wife and that Harry would never fly the little red plane, or any other aircraft, again.

"Maybe God sent you for this plane to give a Christian brother peace about selling it. He knows you'll take good care of it," I assured him.

He nodded thoughtfully, "Yes, maybe so." It wasn't long before I began meeting him at the Kent State Airport for our dates. His fascination with me grew deeper and deeper, yet he always guarded his heart.

Considering the Ring

Every man I met who saw my tattooed wedding band asked me, "Would you ever have it removed?" There was a tone of concern that I wouldn't be able to move forward with my life. It also became clear that they saw it as Don's mark of "ownership" on me. My answer became, "For the right man."

Boaz had been seeing me for almost a year when he asked that same question. As we discussed the possibility of marriage, I decided I should try a slow tattoo removal process. I couldn't afford laser removal; besides, it would have been too drastic for me. Instead, I began a micro-dermal abrasion system. The process would take a while, which was fine by me. I felt pangs of grief each time I applied the cream to my inked finger. I want to do this for the right man. Only he deserved to have his "mark" of commitment on my hand meant for "til death do us part." However, my tattooed cross wedding band is the same now as it was twelve years ago. Maybe God had a different idea about it.

At this one-year mark, just to be sure Boaz was the one, I decided to do a fast—partial, due to hypoglycemia—and pray because I remembered God's message to me in church one morning: "Ask Me, 'Yes or No?' one man at a time. God doesn't look at appearance; instead, He looks at the heart."[14] That's the approach I took after several disheartening dates.

When Boaz and I did our video call, I informed him, "I'm going to fast and pray about our relationship to see if God says you are the one or not. I don't want us to waste each other's time if we aren't right for each other."

Taken back, he admonished me, "That's supposed to be done in secret; otherwise, it's boasting."

"I'm telling you this so you understand how important it is to me. I don't take our relationship lightly. If we date for two or three years, never knowing if God wants us to marry, we've wasted each other's time."

"Oh," he said, "I'll fast and pray too. How long are you doing this?"

"Two weeks."

"Two weeks?" making sure he heard me correctly.

"Yes, I can only do a partial fast because I have hypoglycemia. So, I'm leaving out meat, all drinks except water, and all sweets and snacks," I said. "I also have to function at work," I explained.

"Then, I'll do the same," he agreed.

Two days before our fast ended, I heard in my spirit, "He's the one." When all fourteen days passed, we compared notes: Yes. We both got the same answer and sighed with relief. We hated the midlife dating

---

14   1 Samuel 16:7

scene and were glad our search had ended. Besides, we really did love each other. The in-like part was past. It would have hurt badly if one or both of us got a no from God.

The Proposal

Many people ask the woman for the proposal story when she gets engaged. My late husband, Don, never proposed to me. We just knew we would get married someday. He took me to a local jewelry store to pick out our rings in my senior year of high school. That was it. Nothing grand or romantic as far as that proposal story is concerned for anyone else but me. Boaz, the brilliant man he is, remembered that I'd never had a formal proposal.

On our date weekend, we watched *Safe Haven* on a rented DVD one evening in my living room. It was a girly movie, so I had tears running down my face by the film's end. I'm the kind of woman who cries at girly movies, weddings, baptisms, and baby dedications. Besides, the main character's wife died of cancer. She left him letters in her desk, one of which she said that she prayed for the right woman to come along at the right time for him after her death.

At the end of the movie, Boaz got up from the couch, looking somber, and went upstairs to use the restroom. I thought that either he needed to use the restroom badly, or something was wrong, by the look on his face.

After a few minutes, he came downstairs still looking quite serious. I wondered what was up because he got down on the floor on his hands and knees beside me on the sofa. I thought he might have lost a contact lens and was looking for it. So I bent down to look too. Before I could ask him about it, much to my surprise, a navy blue ring box appeared in front of me as he assumed the "proposal position." When he opened it, revealing the glistening solitaire inside, he asked with blurred concern and fear, "Will you marry me?" I learned later that he'd hoped for a yes, yet worried that I'd say no or he'd have another failed marriage.

Astonished because I thought he wasn't ready for engagement, I said, "Yes!" and cried some more, giving him a big, soggy hug and kiss. He smiled big as he put the ring on my finger. It fit perfectly. We both looked forward to having a committed Christian covenant marriage and spending the rest of our lives together.

THOUGHTS ON THIS CHAPTER

It takes prayerful consideration before dating again as an adult, especially when you are a midlifer or older. It's challenging to know when it's right to start, where to begin, and what your boundaries are. Most of all, it's important to have an understanding of who you are and what you want apart from your identity with your First Blessing. Safeties are a must, so find out from reliable resources what red flags to watch for. I found the book *Date or Soulmate*, written by the founder of e-Harmony, helpful to steer clear of hazardous relationships. Set up a safety net with friends and family when you go out on a date with someone you've never met before to reduce your chances of a tragedy. Also, learn about personality disorders since they are often hidden away like a predator waiting to devour an unsuspecting victim later. Let the Holy Spirit, not your heart, guide you along the way.[15]

Just as Naomi, Ruth, and Orpah had to figure out what to do, where to go, and whether to remarry in Ruth chapter 1, we do too. Maybe you will be like Naomi and decide that finding a husband or wife isn't worth it. Perhaps you will be like Orpah and move back near your family to find love and a new life. Or maybe you will stay connected with your late Love's family while searching for a new love and life. Such decisions must be immersed in prayer to avoid disaster and heartache.

If you choose to find new love, it's critical to ask God about it.[16] Seek wise counsel from a Christian friend, family member, or your pastor. Just as Samuel needed to seek God's approval for choosing the king of Israel, our decision on remarriage should be based on God's "Yes!" It's imperative that we ask God about each date. There is nothing worse than marrying the wrong person. Finding the right Christian spouse to spend the rest of your life is important.

---

15   Jeremiah 17:9
16   1 Samuel 16:7

For Reflection

A number of things emerged in this chapter from my decision to date and whether to remarry:

» Empty place no one else could fill—I loved having my kids and grandkids around, but an emptiness echoed in my heart, one they couldn't fill.

» Decision to date again after so many years—After wondering how to begin dating again, I joined a couple of dating websites. Yet, Internet dating isn't for everyone, that's for sure.

» Learning about yourself—It took me several tries to write my bio. I needed to know who I was and what I wanted from life. Also, I needed to know what qualities I wanted in a potential husband.

» Safety concerns with dating—One had a reputation as a womanizer. I wanted no part of it. Several Christian men had serious issues. One turned out to be a scary online encounter. I had let my adult kids know about my date so if anything went wrong, they knew where I was and who I would meet.

» Knowing your boundaries—Some drank and smoked, some worshipped at St. Mattress, and others thought premarital sex was okay. Christian biblical values were important to me. I wasn't sure what to do as Boaz reached over and confidently took my hand. He stopped, gently swung me around toward him, and kissed me. I didn't know if I should have kissed him back or objected.

» Fear of dishonoring your Love who passed away—I wondered if I was cheating on Don. But I remembered that our vows were "until death we do part."

» Deciding whether to continue dating or not—After a few disheartening dates, I considered giving up.

» Is this the one?—I remembered God saying to me in church one morning, "Ask Me, 'Yes or No?' one man at a time." I told Boaz, "I'm going to fast and pray about our relationship to see if God says you are the one, or not.

Questions for Reflection

1. What qualities did your Love have that you want in a future spouse? What qualities do you not want?

....

....

....

2. What safeties will you put in place as you begin dating again?

....

....

....

3. What boundaries will you set, and how will you maintain them?

....

....

....

4. What red flags will you watch for? What will signal a relationship is worth pursuing?

....

....

....

Scripture for Reflection

• Ruth 1:3-19

....

....

....

- 1 Samuel 16:1-7,11-13

....

....

....

- Isaiah 61:1-3

....

....

....

What other Bible passages or thoughts do you have?

....

....

....

....

....

....

....

....

....

....

....

....

Chapter TEN

Memories Haunt New Relationships

"Why are you doing *this*?" Boaz asked me, visibly irritated. "I feel like you're treating me like someone else!" Seated in his wooden rocker in our living room, he leaned forward, resting on the rocker arms, as frustration stared at me.

Shocked at his response, I stood in the middle of our living room trying to figure out what I had done wrong. *Why does he feel this way?* I wondered. I'd treated him in a manner consistent with Christian marriage, or so I thought. *Did I treat him like Don? Maybe.*

I vowed I would never make comparisons or expect my Boaz to be like Don. But I discovered that was a ridiculous notion. Grieving doesn't stop because the funeral is over, thank-you cards are sent, and you've filed your first set of income taxes as Single/Widowed. Mourning is more than just the loss of a person. It's also the loss of a familiar lifestyle, dreams made with your first Love, holiday traditions, and the thought of growing old together evaporated with the death declaration made by the doctors. *Nothing* will ever be the same again. I will never be the same again.

My Boaz is a wonderful man, but he is not Don. I was beginning to see how different they were. He also had to realize that I was not going to be like his ex-wife. Both of us were in for quite a surprise. Our past expectations butted in without us realizing they even existed. One of those was with our sleep routines.

Past Ghosts Collide with Our Present

As usual, I'd found myself awake around 2:30 a.m. Fibromyalgia had robbed me of my sleep *again*. I quietly slipped out of bed, picked up my smartphone and glasses, then headed into the living room. Since he had to get up early for work, I didn't want to wake him. I started browsing through Pinterest while sitting on our love seat. *Those lights we need for our house are a challenge. We can't agree on what style to choose because our tastes are so different.* Clicking on several links, I saved some I liked, keeping in mind what his mother and sisters had in their homes that he liked. I had to wrap my mind around his Southern upbringing. *Hopefully, I'll get tired enough to sleep again.*

"What are you doing up?" Boaz asked me, sleepy-eyed, when he got up for a restroom trip. He seemed unreasonably concerned by the tone of his voice as he wandered into the living room barefoot and glanced at my phone screen. "When do you think you'll come to bed?"

"When I feel tired enough. Fibro messes with my sleep a lot."

"Please, come back to bed," he pleaded.

"Give me a few more minutes, okay? I need to make myself sleepy." I looked up at him, feeling like I'd stepped on his emotional toes.

"Okay." Looking forlorn, he kissed me, then went back to bed. I joined him a while later and drifted off to sleep.

When we got up for breakfast in the morning, we discussed the previous night. I learned that his ex would spend the entire night on social media, or come tiptoeing in from God knows where in the wee hours of the morning. "She wouldn't come to bed until around the time I got up for work," he lamented. I think he was afraid I might do something similar. We both had to learn each other's sore points to either not trigger them or to work through them. Some issues started heated arguments. It was quite a learning curve for sure.

"Honey. I told you I have fibromyalgia, and getting good, uninterrupted sleep is a common challenge. Please, remember that I love you when I'm up in the middle of the night."

"Okay." He sighed while he finished his breakfast. Then he came over to kiss me where I sat finishing my breakfast at our dining table. "I know you love me. I can't help but worry."

I took his hand in mine and kissed him when he bent down toward me, then gave him a comforting hug. He put on his coat, picked up his keys, wallet, and phone from the counter using his mental ADHD checklist. Then he went out our apartment door. "Bye, Sweetheart. See you tonight. I love you!"

"I love you too. See you tonight."

I found myself walking with him through healing from his past, while he walked with me through my grief.

Two's Company, but More Is a Crowd

On our honeymoon, I'd awakened to my startled new husband. "How *did* your husband die?" He queried.

"I already told you that he died after a long bout with stage 4 colon cancer," I replied.

Boaz said, "I woke up abruptly to your hand in my face with your fingers up my nose!" He demonstrated with his hand on his own face like a large tarantula with its two front legs up his nostrils. "Are you sure he didn't suffocate to death?"

"Seriously? No." I got up to take my shower so we could go to breakfast.

Well, maybe I did what he said? Or was his comment a poor attempt at humor? I pondered the options. I had been enjoying my bed to myself the past couple of years. The cruise ship bed was a full size. Even though we were both smaller built, we were indeed cozy. He would tease me every so often about it and snicker at my eye rolls. *What did I marry?*

***

"Honey, would you switch sides of the bed with me?" I pleaded, with my hand on his shoulder, looking for an agreeable response. I couldn't get comfortable on a different side of my double-sized bed that we now shared.

"I like this side because I get up a couple of times at night to go to the restroom. Besides, my stomach hurts if I lie on my other side," he explained.

It's not like I don't get up too. Sigh. I tossed and turned. *This isn't helping my sleep issues.* Snuggling up against his back, I put my arm around him. He moved my arm awkwardly down his side, putting my shoulder blade in an uncomfortable position. "Your arm is hurting my stomach," he complained.

Rolling over, I tried to make it work. It took time to find what was agreeable for both of us. Eventually, we did by swapping sides of the bed every three or four months. After a few years, we bought a king-size bed, which gives us ample room to lie however we want, and the side of the bed no longer matters.

LOVE FOR . . . TWO?

Sharing a bed also meant learning how to share our bodies with each other. You'd think that making love would be just the two of us. Yet, our bed became extremely crowded in our hearts. Women may have the same anatomy and men may be built the same, yet each individual is unique. Those differences challenged us at first.

"What are you doing?" frustrated, I lost interest and rolled onto my back, staring at a weird textured spot on the ceiling.

"I thought you liked it," he leaned on his side. The way he'd touched me made me uncomfortable. Mentally, my mind flashed back to when I was molested as a little girl.

"No. I don't." I rolled away from him with tears in my eyes. *Don knew what triggers to avoid. Why doesn't Boaz understand me?*

"I'm sorry," he apologized.

"I know." I realized that this would take some time, something neither of us expected.

He leaned over my shoulder to kiss me on the cheek. "Please, don't cry. We'll figure this out." And then he wrapped himself around me.

"You'd think making love would be like riding a bicycle. I guess there's more to it than that." I snuggled into him.

"Maybe we should explore each other without expectations. Would that help?" he offered. We'd been working from what we knew. Exploration could open up new possibilities and intimacy we'd never considered.

So that's what we did. His humor helped too. We needed to learn each other's needs, desires, and expectations. Yet it took time, tears, and hugs for both of us. Eventually, lovemaking became like riding a much different bicycle, learning how to ride smoothly together.

Keeping our bed for just us took work and consideration. Hebrews 13:4 tells us to keep the marital bed pure, which in our case, meant keeping our conversations with each other in mind. We realized that we could talk about ex- and late spouses, but also my abusers outside of the bedroom. This helped us keep our bed to ourselves. Yet other changes took longer for me to accept.

Caged Mouse

I began feeling like a caged mouse. Although Boaz's pet name for me is Mouse, he didn't cause this feeling. The people in the community often made me feel small, like a mouse, unwanted and out of place. I'd left everything I knew and enjoyed where I lived when Boaz met me. None of it was here.

I had tried to get a personal training job in this area just before we married, since I moved into our apartment a couple of months before our wedding. But job hunting proved frustrating. Boaz had his ideas on how I should approach interviews since he was the manager in his department of an automotive supplier and routinely interviewed engineers. The fitness industry is distinctly different from the automotive industry with interviews. He tried to help though.

I quickly realized that I was an Ohio girl in a Michigan world. God allowed me to build a stellar career in Ohio and Pennsylvania that was reflected on my resume. Quickly, the focus in interviews shifted away from how my certifications and expertise could benefit their gym members and clients to an abrupt focus on my Ohio background and the superiority of the personal training manager's credentials. "So you're from *Ohio*? You worked in Pennsylvania for a while?"

In one gym, I sat through the personal training manager bragging on his accomplishments in bodybuilding and Ironman competitions. It seemed like he wanted me to feel "less than" as a fitness professional. In my mind, I'd already decided to move on to another gym interview.

"How *did* you get such an incredible resume?" I felt like my integrity was under intense scrutiny in yet another interview.

"You have a lot of certifications. How did you get *all* of those?" queried the personal training manager in the last interview I endured.

After so many "I'll call you" promises, my hopes of staying in the career I loved vanished. I could get a gym job almost two hours away from our home in the Detroit metroplex, but I'd have to work for free to build up my client base. I'd already paid my dues years ago doing free stuff. Driving that far for free didn't make sense. Long commutes and a full day's work also don't go well with fibromyalgia. I went from training clients and helping gym members every day, all day, to nothing. God had provided all my previous gym jobs, why won't He give me one now?

Depressed, I tried to find a job in a local store or office. Nope.

Boaz would go out my cage door at 4:30 a.m. and return around 6:30 p.m., rescuing me from my loneliness. We would go out for a while in the evenings, and I'd drive to meet him near his work to have lunch with him for our Friday date day. People's attitudes in the community had built my cage of isolation, not him. *"Oh, you poor thing! Sitting around in your apartment all day, day in and day out!"* a woman at church exclaimed. She could see my dilemma, but be a friend? Nope. The silent message was loud and clear: I wasn't from around here. It was as if I were a ghost moving about the community. It wasn't until about three years later that I finally made a couple of friends.

***

Boaz inadvertently contributed to my caged-ness, although he didn't build it. He was ultra frugal, insisting on my being ultra frugal too and highly accountable to him. I had to give him a list of the bills and other expenses I was responsible for paying, the grocery budget, and my spending money. He scrutinized them. It all seemed reasonable, but there was a hitch. It seemed that he didn't share his total budget with me, claiming that as long as our accounts were in the positive, he was fine. He didn't give me the same accountability for his spending as he expected from me, creating a double standard. Sure, he earned the money to pay the bills, which I didn't take for granted. I was used to more of a partnership style of marriage.

Boaz transferred the money into a checking account with our names on it that I used to pay bills and buy groceries, but he frequently forgot to put money into my account due to his ADHD. There was nothing more embarrassing than having my debit card declined and for the store to hold my groceries in a stock room cooler until he finally transferred the money. "I'm sorry, but my husband must have forgotten to transfer money into our bill account. Can you hold these for me? I'll call him and come back to pay for them."

"Uh, sure." The cashier waved the head cashier over to cancel the transaction before a bagger wheeled my cart of bagged groceries back to the stock room. The eye rolls, side glances, and uh-huhs denoted suspicion as the head cashier voided my transaction and called a bagger to retrieve my groceries. It probably didn't help my chances for getting a job there either.

Eventually, I learned that his ex ran up huge credit card balances. I wasn't like her. I had managed our family's tight finances when Don was alive as a thrifty money manager—the other end of the frugal scale. It took quite a while for him to trust me with transferring the funds myself and letting him know how much and what it covered. I wasn't like his ex, which he learned over time. Yet I needed to respect his frugalness while he needed to honor my past money management skills on such a tight budget.[17]

This mouse struggled in her cage of isolation to make a life in a rural, multi-generational community closed to "outsiders." I longed to live in a place where I was liked and respected, where I felt free to be me. That struggle showed up at church as well.

BIG SHIFTS

I remember first sitting in the sanctuary of Boaz's church, which he attended when he met me. As the service opened, I picked up the hymnal from the rack in front of me. The worship leader beamed proudly as he waved his hands, leading the musicians, choir, and congregation in hymns. *Only hymns.* I preferred a blend of hymns and contemporary worship music. A trumpet player, with an air of superiority, trilled along on the song's obbligato line. The atmosphere didn't seem worshipful to me.

After congregational singing, we sat back down and obediently opened our Bibles. A gentleman read the featured Bible passage from his King James Bible with a worn black leather cover. *Hmmm. I'm glad I have my NKJV. At least, it's tolerated in KJV-preferred churches.* The pastor came up to the pulpit on the stark platform with blue carpet. As he railed against the latest sin issues in our country, he became increasingly agitated. His intense volume made my temples pound as my headache competed with him for my attention. When the service was over, I wondered how attached Boaz was to that church.

---

17   Ephesians 5:22-30; Colossians 3:18-19

After a few head-pounding weeks, I asked," Does the pastor always preach against contemporary sin issues and world events? It seems that he's more about preaching the news than God's Word. He also seems bent on condemning Americans and guilting the congregation to come forward for salvation or re-dedication."

He sighed, "I didn't pick this church. My ex did. I stayed because I'd made friends here and the Bible teaching in Sunday school is really good. They were also supportive of me when she left."

"I see. You know the church I came from. Is there a church more like it that wouldn't give me headaches?" I hoped I didn't offend him, but I couldn't do one more Sunday there. Besides, he seemed to like my church back in Northeast Ohio. A conservative, Bible-teaching church with a contemporary style, something along those lines seemed like the better option for us.

"Sure," he agreed.

It took a few visits to different churches in the area, but then he remembered one he'd attended long before he met me. It was a good fit for both of us—not what I was used to, but we felt comfortable with the service style of blended worship music and solid Sunday school teaching. We needed a church where we both were spiritually fed and could genuinely worship God. This one did, but it still held a lot of the common small-town issues that gave me flashbacks to two troubled churches where Don and I served in ministry. Adjusting took time.

A Shoe Fling

Adjusting to our daily living habits took time too. One day, I tripped over his shoes—again. He'd left them in the walkway right in front of the entry door of our house-in-process. I decided to put a mat by the door that opened into the garage and placed all of our shoes on it as a safe shoe space. Maybe this would help with his ADHD-ness.

"What's this?" Boaz barked at me, pointing to our new shoe space when he saw it.

"I kept tripping over your shoes you left in front of the door, so I set a mat away from it to put our shoes," I replied.

He moved his shoes off the mat back where they were, "I don't like it. By the way, you have too many shoes. I don't have a place to put mine."

"There is room for yours too. I only have two pair here. Three pair will fit. Why did you leave them in the middle of the walkway? I tripped over them. I could have broken my neck!" I replied.

"I didn't!" he denied tersely, as he strolled into the kitchen.

I walked over and placed his shoes on the mat. "I want to keep our house neat *and* safe."

He followed me and promptly plopped them back where he'd left them earlier, which still I thought was a terrible spot.

"No," I stated firmly putting them back on the mat. I wasn't a pushover and refused to be one now.

He bellowed, "Forget this! Let's just eliminate some of your shoes!" He picked my tennis shoes up, opened the door to the garage, and hurled them out into the sea of tools, building supplies, and other stuff. They disappeared among his piles.

"Fine!" I yelled, picked his shoes up, and flung them into the garage. *By golly, two can play this game. I'm fed up with this ridiculous behavior!* I just wanted order out of the chaos that comes with his neurodiversity. Supposedly, he was organized and tidy. Not. I'd endured ADHD clutter messes—aka squirrel stashes—for a good portion of my life with my family and late husband, and I was *done* with it.

He glared at me for a moment, seemingly not knowing what to do with someone who stands her ground. Don left his stuff everywhere, but he worked with me. I didn't get the pushback from him that I got with Boaz.

When we got into arguments, they were doozies. Not long after we officially moved into the portion of our house that we finished, we found ourselves wrangling with territory struggles and drawing battle lines. We discovered that we weren't willing to make some changes or let the other one in on our decision-making. *Is he just being stubborn?* I often wondered. *Am I? Why is this so difficult?*

The man I'd married was still the man I fell in love with. We did indeed love each other and God had brought us together. I just hadn't encountered this side of him until now. I also didn't realize some of my issues deep down that I'd picked up as a little girl growing up in such family dysfunction would surface like they did. I refused to resort to those tactics, which the shoe-flinging match sparked in my mind. I'd never dealt with that kind of conflict with Don. Maybe it was because we had practically grown up together in high school and matured together while we were young. Sure, we had our issues, but not like this.

We both agreed we needed help navigating our challenges since we felt stuck, unable to shift our emotional gears. So we decided to meet with a Christian marriage counselor to deal with our difficulties. With her, we learned to communicate better and consider each other's wants and needs that were different from what we were used to. We learned that as older newlyweds we had become entrenched in habits that needed to be renegotiated in our remarriage. Working toward solutions was much better than fighting to win. Wise counsel helped us learn better ways to deal with conflict and grow closer.[18]

We found that regular dates and annual "honeymoons"—aka anniversary trips—helped us pull together as one. We love exploring together, whether finding a new bike trail, taking the Michigan Lighthouse Circle Tour, wandering Frankenmuth, or exploring the Bay City area. He took me places I never thought I would see, like Hawaii, London, and Israel. We also spent enjoyable time together as we worked on our home in the evenings. It was just the two of us together looking forward to what the future might bring. Slowly the ties that bind, as symbolized in our Cord of Three Strands that we braided during our wedding ceremony, started growing lovingly together—and our smiles reflected it.

18   Proverbs 1:5

THOUGHTS ON THIS CHAPTER

Pulling two separate lives into one can be much like iron sharpening iron.[19] Sparks will fly. How you handle ghosts of the past, differences, disappointments, and disagreements can pull you into greater oneness or drive a wedge between the two of you. The divorce rate for remarriage is 65 percent. I'm sure that twice-blessed couples don't want to become part of that statistic.[20] It doesn't mean you don't love each other or that you were duped by a false persona from your Second Blessing. It simply means you get to see their everyday version instead of looking through the rose-colored, heart-shaped lenses of infatuation.

I want to give you a word of caution: If you feel in danger with your new Love, by all means, go to a safe place such as the police, a domestic violence shelter, or a friend or family member who can help you. Don't allow yourself to be abused. I've encountered women who had been beaten by their second Love and had to flee the relationship. That's not God's design for marriage.

Past issues can dominate your relationship, but they don't have to. It takes recognizing what interferes with your life together. You may want a Christian counselor or your pastor to help sort issues out and guide you both to work for solutions rather than fight to win. Disagreements are normal and healthy, but fighting is not. We meet with our counselor for annual Christian marital wellness check-ups. We can manage any issues that may be brewing but also celebrate our victories together. It's definitely worth the investment for a lifelong love relationship.

---

19   Proverbs 27:17

20   Larry F. Waldman, PhD, ABPP, "Five Reasons Why Second Marriage Might Fail at a High Rate," Find a Psychologist (website), accessed 06/30/2025, https://www.findapsychologist.org/five-reasons-why-second-marriages-might-fail-at-a-high-rate-by-dr-larry-waldman/.

These are several points where the first marriage, our pasts, and our new marriage collided:

» Not recognizing and appreciating each Love's personality— "Why are you treating me like this?"
» The struggle to find sexual compatibility and mutual satisfaction—You'd think making love would be like riding a bicycle, but there's more to it than that.
» Financial differences and expectations—He expected me to be highly accountable with funds, but he didn't follow the same expectations that he had of me.
» The one who moves often loses the most—I felt small and restricted, an outsider where we lived. My church style wasn't available where we lived. I couldn't find a job in my career field the way I had expected.
» Territorial challenges—Our shoe-flinging contest is a fine example of this issue.

Questions for Reflection

1. What died along with your first Sweetheart?

....

....

....

2. If you've found someone, what issues hamper your relationship? If not, what are you willing to change, but what do you refuse to change?

....

....

....

3. If you've remarried, what do you and your Love say is working well, and what is not? If not, what are some of your expectations for remarriage?

4. Do you both believe God brought you together? How can your past interfere with your present relationship?

5. What do you have to work through so you can move forward in your life together?

6. If you've chosen to remarry, how can you please each other? How can you consider each other's needs and interests with your own, while remaining focused on Christ?

7. How can you protect your marital bed from becoming overcrowded with ex-spouses and dead loves?

Scripture for Reflection

- Luke 9:59-62

- 1 Corinthians 7:32-40

....

....

....

- Hebrews 13:4

....

....

....

Do you have any other Bible passages or thoughts?

....

....

....

....

....

....

....

....

....

....

....

....

....

....

....

....

Chapter ELEVEN

The House that Love Built

Why can't we just melt the ice and be done with it?" I whined as I picked up the umpteenth frozen chunk from the basement of our house in process. What a miserable, awful mess!

Boaz kept chipping away with ice shards flying everywhere. "Because if we don't, we could lose thousands of dollars—the tools, heat pump, water softener, furnace, and everything else in here." He stood up to stretch out his aching back. "Besides, how would we remove all the water from the basement? The best way is to chip away at it and remove it in chunks," he stated in a matter-of-fact tone.

Chip. Dig. Haul. Chip. Dig. Haul. *Ugh!*

The outdoor temperatures had plummeted to minus 30 degrees in the Thumb of Michigan with the winter's brutal polar vortex. Even though we wrapped heat tape and insulation around the sump pump pipe, it wasn't enough to withstand such frigid temperatures. The water on the outside of the pipe began to freeze, causing water to spray back into the basement of our house, which he hadn't yet connected to the heating system. Everything was encased in ice. The floor was coated in about five inches or more of the frozen, slippery stuff. We found ourselves dealing with that horrendous mess on the first Saturday of spring.

As I continued to slip and slide on the melting ice, I bent over by the furnace to pick up a sizable ice chunk. In front of my face was a small black and orange butterfly. I wondered if it was alive or if it had died with its tiny feet frozen to that ice chunk. When I blew on it gently, the butterfly's wings spread out to display its gorgeous orangey-red design on its lovely black cloak.

I carefully carried it up the steps and set it gently on the ice pile. After a few minutes, the butterfly flew away. What a beautiful sign of hope amid our mess.

Our relationship became durable as we navigated challenges together. The reality of remarried love was revealed when the rose color of infatuation drained from our heart-shaped lenses. Now we could see each other more clearly. We then began to understand that remarriage in midlife has quirks, unfulfilled dreams, and unspoken expectations. This house represented much of our stretching, growing, and letting go to move forward, all that needed to happen in our mid-life remarriage. Here, we could begin building oneness with Jesus at the center.

IN THE REARVIEW MIRROR

One day, an old model pickup truck rolled up our long, winding driveway, leaving a dust cloud in its wake. I stepped out of our makeshift camper-workstation to see who'd come to visit. Our life-worn farmer-neighbor climbed out and greeted me as he shut his door. "Hi, Char. How's it going?"

"Hi, Dale. Going well, but slow. How are you?"

"Good. Can't complain. Yeah, I know. It's been under construction for a long time." He tilted his ball cap back, wiping some sweat off his forehead on that mid-summer day.

"How long?" He piqued my curiosity as the late morning sun threatened to be a scorcher.

"Boaz began construction on this house with his ex-wife and two kids after they moved here in the Thumb of Michigan—that's why it's nicknamed the Mitten State," he demonstrated the geography with his hand. "After he lived a few years in the Chicago area near where he worked, he bought some of my land when I decided to downsize my farm."

This purchase made them close neighbors. Boaz told me he'd chosen this area when his job brought him to the Detroit metroplex because he wanted to live in a rural community. Finding a great municipal airport nearby for his love of aviation had sealed the deal in his heart. When he saw the Acreage For Sale sign, he talked with Dale about purchasing the back forty acres and building a house on the front portion, several yards behind the farmer's home.

I learned that Dale and his wife had watched Boaz's family fly apart over time. Disheartened after he completed the shell of the house, Boaz lost his family and his desire to work on the house he had lovingly begun to build for them. His first wife had pointed out a house that was the same as a plan he liked, but they would never enjoy living there together. He could only link the house to his family because his son had helped with its construction, hoping his son would live there someday.

Boaz worked on it here and there, building this dream house. But the fuel that stoked the fire in his heart to work on it in the evenings evaporated. One evening, Dale had looked out his kitchen window with his wife to see Boaz standing outside the framed structure, tears streaming down his face. His only reprieve from the pain of his shattered family and dreams was soaring through the sky in his single-engine plane as often as possible. Boaz believed people can't hurt you when you're up high above the pain, alone with God. The house shell stood waiting for a family to love it into a home.

During his break from building the house, Boaz later shared, he had carefully selected some internet dating websites to join. He thought he should cast his net wide for a wife who would love and cherish him—ADHD and all. After several disappointing dates, he came home for dinner one evening after work and began to sort through his matches. One site seemed promising as he scanned his inbox, finding a match that stood out. It popped up with an intriguing profile. *She's a Christian, doesn't smoke or drink, and is a personal trainer. She's a widow of a pastor—and cycles on trails!* he noted. He immediately began typing a message to me with great enthusiasm and then waited somewhat impatiently for my response. Of course, you know the rest of the story.

TITANIUM STRONG

Boaz bought a titanium wedding ring set with a premium-quality cubic zirconia solitaire for me.

"I chose this set because of your work in the gym."

At first, I thought, *Why didn't he get a diamond engagement ring? A small stone is fine, nothing fancy—a basic solitaire. Maybe he got it because he was afraid our marriage wouldn't last.*

I later discovered that he worried about the diamond getting knocked out of a softer gold setting, and the cost of replacing it led to his decision. I began appreciating his practical approach as I picked up weights to re-rack them in the gym. *Whoa. I could have knocked the stone out of the setting. It's good that this isn't a gold band with an expensive diamond.* Other brides had to insure their rings and file claims for lost stones. Not me. I also later learned that he appreciated my insistence on wearing matching wedding bands. He'd never had that before.

During our wedding ceremony, I noticed a tear trickle down his cheek. I remembered at the altar what he had told me during our dating time: "I feel like I have a Christmas present, but I don't know what it is yet." What he told me later was he knows people change, but how would I change? Would I be willing to fight for our marriage if necessary. *Would he want to keep me?*

"It's Christmas," I whispered to him as the pastor held up our rings and talked about the traditional symbolism behind them. Afterward, we braided our Cord of Three Strands to symbolize our union with Christ, binding us together as one. That photo as my smartphone background still greets me today.

Little did I know that my ring and this house symbolized our marriage. Ghosts of our pasts and the level of his adult ADHD challenged us. Yet, because of our faith in Jesus Christ, we eventually built oneness. It took time, effort, and patience.

Love Nest Struggles

After we married, I began to help finish this home, which had quite a while to go in the building process. It was a design I wouldn't have chosen, even though it was a stunning, grand, Georgian Revival home. It had elements of his ex-wife's influence I wouldn't have picked. I also found out he had definite ideas about the décor of this Georgian home, disregarding my opinion. I soon discovered there really wasn't room for me to put some of my own touches on it. It would be his house, and I would get to live in it.

Tension built shortly after we unpacked our bags from our honeymoon. I'd endured temporary living situations way too often as a child and in my first marriage due to Don's jobs and pastoral ministry. I was way beyond ready to settle into our home now—not years later. We argued often about it. What tipped the scales to get it finished a bit sooner was when I became extremely ill from mold exposure in our apartment.

"Hello. This is Charlaine Martin in apartment 202, building H." Our closet ceiling had a leak. "It's bad," I told the manager on the phone.

"I'm sorry that happened to you, Mrs. Martin. I'll call the roofer to check it out."

After several follow-up calls, I learned that the roofer couldn't get up there to fix it for a few weeks because there was so much snow on the roof. When we discovered this leak, I moved our clothes and shoes to another closet, placed a bucket under the drip, and set up a fan for air circulation.

The mold still grew. My heart rate and blood pressure plummeted, and my body hurt so badly, while I felt overwhelming exhaustion. A rheumatologist diagnosed me with a systemic autoimmune disease. Boaz pushed through the building process by hiring out a couple of the projects to subcontractors. Although the apartment building's roof was fixed, the ceiling in our apartment was not. Mold was in several buildings, as I discovered when the apartment management company systematically re-roofed the buildings in our complex. The mildew smell in the air pinned me to our couch in misery. So, I began spending more time at our house in process and in the camper during the day, waiting for Boaz to come home so we could work on it. Even then, I could barely function.

God must have heard my prayers because Boaz finally relented on some of my wishes. He purchased some beautiful Tiffany-style lights at a local DIY store—on sale, no less. The great price appealed to his frugalness, and I felt more part of our home. He also entrusted me with designing our kitchen cabinets. Although we didn't always agree on everything, we gave it the look that goes along with such a grand home. Once he let me in to help pull the house together, we grew closer in our relationship.

Giving Back

One day, after we had moved in, I looked out the front window of the house to see a rainbow almost a full circle framing our neighbors' home. "Boaz, come here and see this!" I called out.

He met me by the window to see what had my attention. "Interesting. It's right over Dale's house."

"Yes, it is. What's God up to?'

Our farmer-neighbor had been diagnosed with colorectal cancer earlier that year, a common malady for the farming community. I cringed when his family told us about it. All the emotions I felt with Don's cancer journey flooded back. I could feel my eyes sting with tears as I tried to stifle them in front of Dale and his family. We committed to praying for his healing and his family's strength and provision. I gave his wife website links to resources I found helpful in searching for help to manage the exorbitant bills that would flood their mailbox. Unfortunately, she believed they had good health insurance so she didn't follow through on finding help for the costs they would inevitably pay out of pocket. They tried all the known treatments plus some experimental ones and still failed to get his late-stage cancer to back down. I was afraid we would see him in his casket at the funeral home in town.

"Let's show it to them," Boaz insisted.

"Yes, let's do," I agreed.

We knocked on their door and got them to come out. They saw the rainbow, but wanted to see it from our perspective. Dale's daughter helped him get in his truck and drove him back in front of our house.

"By golly, you're right!" he exclaimed in a stifled tone.

"God's telling you something, I think," I looked at him to see what he thought. He and his family were believers.

"Maybe it's for healing," he pondered aloud.

"Maybe. All I know is that the rainbow in the Bible is a symbol of hope. It might be hope."

"I think you're right," he said thoughtfully.

"Yes, Dad. God is giving you hope." His daughter encouraged him with a tearful smile.

Within three months of seeing the rainbow, as I expected, we stood in the funeral home by his casket, knowing Dale was Home. Hope helped him go through the process of going Home.

Hope helped his wife and daughter land softly in a more afforadable home, when the bank foreclosed on their farm house. It was easier for them to maintain too. As I said earlier about Don's death, death for believers is a different kind of healing. For the following year, we checked in on his widow and daughter. It hurt, but I understood what they were going through. God reminded me how much others had ministered to me in my journey with Don's cancer and eventual Homegoing. How could I not support and encourage them, having gone through the same experiences?[21]

BECOMING ONE IS A PROCESS

Becoming one as a couple, symbolized by the Cord of Three Strands we braided together, meant more than saying, "I do." I think of the "leave and cleave" Bible passage in Genesis 2:24 ESV,

"Therefore a man shall leave his father and his mother and hold fast to his wife, and they shall become one flesh."

It involved letting go of our personal dreams, expectations, and anything that could get in the way so we could begin to dream together—building oneness.

It involved helping my Boaz learn how to be the type of spiritual leader in the home God intended for me. How Don led me as my first husband worked well. Although I was willing to adjust, I decided to show Boaz how to lead me in the way I follow best—through influence and mutual submission, as equal partners. I needed to follow Boaz's lead, but I needed him to lead me in a way that made it easier to follow him as the spiritual leader in our home.[22]

Over my early years with Boaz, I remembered that God had called me to write just a few months before Don's death. Due to my new location and my health conditions, now I couldn't work in a gym, so Boaz encouraged me to follow that call and has supported my writing ministry ever since. Maybe God withheld a gym job from me to fulfill His call for me to write, but also to become the wife Boaz needed. He felt that God called us together as partners in ministry for several reasons, this being one of them. I couldn't agree more.

Boaz built a writing nook for me by a bedroom window. It was there that I started this God-adventure in writing. The nice thing about it is that writing is quite portable. I can pack up my computer and smartphone to write in the car, in a hotel room, or in a family member's spare room. God gave me a renewed purpose since He withheld a gym

---

21   2 Corinthians 1:3-4

22   Colossians 3:18-19,; Ephesians 5:22-24

job in our area and gave me the opportunity to follow His call to write. It also helped Boaz connect with me on a deeper spiritual level as we discuss my writing projects together.

HEADED SOUTH

Funding our retirement dream meant selling the land around our home and then, later, our Michigan home. It costs too much money, but also time and energy to maintain two properties. Also, stocks in pharmaceutical companies during COVID-19 helped make it happen. We found an airpark in Central Florida where we could dream our retirement home together, and he could have a hangar for his airplane attached to it in a warmer, sunny climate for our sunset years.

Even with our seven-year age difference, my illness caused us to age at a similar rate. Our health conditions made cold weather harmful, which meant moving to a place that doesn't plunge to negative degrees in the winter. So, at the end of the COVID-19 pandemic, we built our dream home. We chose the home plan, colors, and décor we liked together. He made several compromises so I could have what I wanted too.

Our new home contained elements from each of us because we chose everything together from the start. We selected the home plan and the crystal chandeliers for the formal areas, while I brought in the Tiffany-style lights he bought for me from our previous house. He has his airplanes in his hanger, while I have a modest pool and front porch. We each feel a part of our home.

There were chapters in our lives that had to close to open the one titled "Us." We each needed to let go so God could take control. Our seven-year incubation period ended, and we gelled together more and more.

***

A surprise came when Boaz's son, who helped work on the beginning of the house in Michigan, bought it for his family. He planned to continue building the rest of the house plan. We handed the house keys to him to continue the family legacy of Boaz's original dream house. They would certainly love it into their new home well.

After the last box went into the moving truck, we headed out for our long drive south. No looking back. Now we were free to be one as God intended for us all along. When we arrived at our new home, I reminded him that he never carried me over the threshold of the Michigan house. I must confess that we staged the threshold carry because he damaged his shoulder moving heavy boxes down a ladder, and one slid backward, injuring his rotator cuff. We set up one of our smartphones on a tripod to video the event from inside the house.

We stepped back outside and closed the door. Then he picked me up, I reached down to open the door, and he carried me inside. "Honey, we're home!" I exclaimed. Immediately, I hopped down to protect his shoulder and back.

"We sure are!" he agreed, both of us beaming as we sealed the moment with a kiss.

We could now begin our new chapter in retirement. We were excited and nervous at the same time, but we now have a home—and a life—that was meant for us.

THOUGHTS ON THIS CHAPTER

It's not unusual for Twice Blessed couples to clash on styles of what they want in their homes and their furnishings. Sometimes one will move into the other's existing home, trying to find space to belong. If both lost their Sweethearts, it's difficult for the ones moving in to be welcome to make changes so they feel at home. The one whose house is to become their love nest may feel invaded, or the memory of their late spouse violated when changes are made.

I've met Twice Blessed couples who foresaw problems and bought a home that was solely theirs. Even then, styles, opinions, and each one's belongings caused tension. I came with furnishings, kitchenware, and more for us, so he didn't have to get anything out of storage. We used what I had until we decided to replace some items, so it reflected us more. Whatever you and your Second Blessing choose to do, keeping each other in mind when making choices together is important for oneness as a couple.[23]

We also discovered that God gives us the opportunity to offer support to other couples going through long-term terminal illness and the grief that follows. He calls us to comfort each other with the same comfort we have been given from 2 Corinthians 1:3–4. It's bittersweet to walk with others as we remember our own pain. Being open to walking through others' grief with them will also help you with yours.

For Reflection

There are several things in this chapter that widows and widowers go through when they choose to remarry:

» Holding onto the past—Boaz's emotional attachment to the house in process while I looked forward to having a home and design elements I liked.

23   Philippians 2:4

» Difficulty changing in midlife and older—Recognizing that rigidity was harming our remarriage, we often argued about what we wanted with our home during the process. He eventually relented and allowed me to make some choices.

» Finding hope amid their remarriage struggles—The butterfly represented hope to me since the Michigan house was a source of contention for Boaz and me. The rainbow respresented hope for Dale's family, revealing it to us to share with them.

» Transition from infatuation to married love—The rose-color drained from our heart-shaped lenses to reveal the reality of remarried love. We'd become titanium strong.

» Getting perspective from others to understand our Loves—Dale and Boaz shared the backstory of the Michigan house. Boaz's son eventually bought this house from us, freeing us to move to Central Florida since paying for and maintain two homes cost too much.

» We made sacrifices for each other—I helped remove the ice from the basement, Boaz worked harder to finish the house when I became ill, and we chose the design elements for both homes together.

» Ministering to others who experience what we've experienced—Encouraging our farmer-neighbor and his family when we learned of his cancer, showing them the hope God gave them through the rainbow He used to frame their house, and checking on his widow and daughter the year right after his death.

Questions for Reflection

1. What is hard for you to let go of so you can bond better with your Second Blessing?

....

....

....

....

2. What is important to each of you for your future together?

....

....

....

3. Whose home will you (or did you) move into after you married? If not, what would you need to feel at home together with your Boaz (or Ruth)?

....

....

....

4. Who has God brought across your path who needs your support and encouragement through a similar journey you've already navigated?

....

....

....

5. How has (or is) God shown up in this phase of your Twice Blessed marriage?

....

....

....

6. What obstacles to oneness is God removing in your Twice Blessed marriage?

....

....

....

Scripture for Reflection

- Ecclesiastes 4:9-12

- Ephesians 5:22-31

- Proverbs 18:22

- 2 Corinthians 1:3-4

Any other Bible passage or thoughts?

Chapter
TWELVE

Two Valentines
=
Doubly Blessed

While sipping my coffee this morning, I was drawn to tears as I browsed through Facebook. One of my posts from a few years ago in the "On This Day" at the top of my newsfeed painfully reminded me about a time of intense sorrow shortly after my first husband's death. Surrealness crept into my memory as my breath stopped for a moment. It was the Valentine's Day gift I had inadvertently given him a few months after his death. I remember avoiding the thought of my first Valentine's Day without him. Naively attempting to ignore the holiday altogether to alleviate my heart's loss of my high school sweetheart hadn't worked. Tears trickled down my cheeks while I stared at the post, frozen. My mind drifted back to our first Valentine's Day as a married couple.

PRAYER MATCHMAKERS

We married young while we were both in college. Our hearts fluttered in our newlywed bliss. This event answered two little elderly ladies' prayers, whom we knew from the small town where we grew up. We had no idea of this match made in heaven until we discovered their spiritual matchmaking years after our "I do's."

"Don and Char!" Edith's eyes twinkled as a smile spread across her age-etched face. Dorothy turned from putting cash in the money box from another rummage sale customer.

"Well, hello!" She beamed. Her white hair and warm heart were exactly as I remembered them from my youth.

"It's good to see you both," Don replied. We placed children's clothing for our preschool son and toddler daughter on the makeshift checkout counter and baby clothes for our pre-born daughter, who was still growing in my belly.

"We'd always prayed the two of you would get together," Edith said. Her smile revealed her delight to see their answered prayers standing in front of them. Dorothy nodded in agreement.

Astonished, we thanked them for their prayers as we caught up with them briefly and gave them the payment for our thrifting finds, supporting missions through the church.

Celebrating Newlywed Love

Just a few months into our first year as Mr. and Mrs., Valentine's cards and gifts flooded the store where I worked as a cashier. I loved the bright reds, pinks, and purples that adorned the store's gift aisle. Love was certainly in the air, according to the greeting card companies. Don and I had gifted each other with Valentine's cards and fun gifts since I was sixteen. Our first Valentine's Day was special because we had recently sealed our love with our vows and rings before God in our hometown church.

***

I remember that holiday as if it were yesterday. Don, a romantic at heart, hurried to the local grocery store, searching for the perfect gift to express his love for me. Later, he shared the story with me, this scene as my mind's eye pictured it.

The store's floral department greeted Don with brilliantly colored roses for the occasion. Some were elaborate bouquets, while others stood gracefully solo in pretty glass vases, each adorned with a satin bow.

The array of choices was overwhelming. Limited by our meager funds, Don browsed the displays until he found something within our budget. With great thought, he selected a fresh pink rose for me. A big grin spread across his face.

"I'd like that one," he said to the woman behind the counter, pointing it out.

The store clerk wrapped it with care in the floral paper. She handed him the gift-wrapped rose as he slid the money across the counter to her.

He left the store with a sparkle in his eyes. "Won't Char be surprised to find this after she gets off work!" The Valentine's Day rose lay beautifully packaged in the passenger seat of his rusty green hatchback as he drove down the wintery-slushed streets.

Don pulled my spare key out of his coat pocket, trying not to drop it in the snow of the store's parking lot. Smiling, he opened the door of my car. He tried to place the prized rose on my steering wheel, but it perplexed him to find the best way to weave the stem through the grip so it would stay put. With a final sigh, he perched it on the steering wheel so I would find it waiting for me after work.

Meanwhile, I was busy inside with last-minute holiday shoppers. He then hurried home to wait for me, anticipating hugs and kisses interlaced with, "Oh, thank you!"

DISAPPOINTMENT COULDN'T EXTINGUISH LOVE

I could see my breath ahead of me in the frigid air as I hurried to my car after the manager locked the store's doors. Snowflakes fluttered in the night sky while parking lot lamps spotlighted their wintery dance. I carried a bag with a small box of Don's favorite chocolates and a big Valentine's Day card I'd bought for him during my lunch break. I quickly slipped into my car, started it, and drove home cautiously on the slick streets. My heart overflowed with excitement.

Once home, I trotted up the stairs and stepped inside our apartment. "Hi, Hon," I greeted Don as I set my bag on a nearby chair and removed my snow-glittered coat. Don sat relaxed on the sofa, facing the door to see me come in. He inquired with a full-face smile, "Hi! Well?"

"Uh, well, what?" I responded with a raised eyebrow, concerned that I might have forgotten something he wanted me to pick up, like milk at the grocery store.

"Hmmm. Did you find your Valentine's Day gift?" Concern mounted in his voice.

"No. Why?" I hesitated as I stood there, wondering what his concern might be.

"*Oh, no!* It was on your car's steering wheel." He groaned as he sprang to his feet and pulled on his coat. He grabbed my spare keys from the coffee table and dashed out our apartment door.

After a few minutes, Don returned from the parking lot with a smooshed pink rose. It looked pitiful as it dripped dirty, melted snow, with its pretty wrapping soiled by my boots. In an air of disappointment, he gave it to me with a hug and kiss. "I was afraid it might fall off your steering wheel. I just wanted to surprise you. Happy Valentine's Day! I love you so much!"

"I know you do. I love you too! It looks beautiful." I took it carefully from him and tried to revive the poor, bedraggled gift of love. We exchanged cards with lots of hugs and kisses. Spending the rest of the evening together at home was so lovely.

***

Sitting in front of my computer gazing at that Facebook post, I continued reminiscing over the years of our marriage. We enjoyed giving each other fun love offerings like corny, pun-filled cards. We read them together, snickering as we snuggled. There were other interesting gifts, like a funny-looking stuffed creature he gave me one year. When I pressed the heart in its hand, it played a cheesy rendition of "Love Will Keep Us Together." It occurred to me that some of our gifts were a bit hokey, but what mattered to us was the love we shared.

Death Can't Kill Love

Then I wandered deeper into that Facebook memory which drew me back to the more recent past. During the difficult year following Don's death, I had mostly ignored the pink, red, and purple heart decorations in the local stores. Seriously, I didn't want to think about it. On the particular evening of that post, I'd arrived home from my workday at the health club with sore, achy legs. The apartment had an eerie emptiness while I removed my coat and boots. My plump, fluffy cat wound around my feet, purring as if to say, "Welcome home!" I smiled as I pet his soft, vibrating head. He helped make me feel at home. Then I sank into the large, comfy sofa with my laptop to check my email.

One, in particular, grabbed my attention. I hesitated at first with a deep sigh, finger poised over the mouse button. Finally, I clicked to open it. It was the monument company I'd contacted a few days earlier.

The email requested that I finalize the last detail for Don's burial place. I found a contract attached with a design awaiting my approval. Since it required a prompt response, I replied matter-of-factly that it looked fine, giving them my okay to proceed with the plan. Mechanically, I printed out the contract, scribbled my signature, and put it in a stamped envelope to mail back the next day.

Numb, I sat on the couch, suddenly realizing it was Valentine's Day. The flood gates opened, and my eyes gushed tears as grief washed over me. I remembered our Valentine's Days together. No more surprising each other with fun cards or cute gifts. No more snuggles and giggles. Instead, I was haunted by the last time we cuddled in his hospital bed after all the tubes and wires had been removed from his cancer-wracked body. This took place the day before he left for a brief stay in hospice.

No more cuddle time together this year or any other, for that matter. It felt like my heart was ripped out of my chest. I curled up with a pillow and my cat, sobbing.

"Mrrrow?" Morris, my cuddly feline purred, nuzzling under my arm.

How crazy it seemed that I had given Don a lovely gray headstone with the best picture of him I could find neatly fixed on the stone's face for his grave. My Facebook post that day said, "What a very odd Valentine's Day. I just signed the contract for Don's headstone." It was the final act of love I could show him on Valentine's Day.

LOVING TWO MEN

As I reflect on those pain-filled times, I realize how blessed I'd been to share so much love with Don for almost thirty years. Yet, I also find myself grateful for Boaz, my Second Blessing whom God brought into my life. We now celebrate Valentine's together, among many other holidays, with our own traditions. How odd it is to love two men—one dead and one living.

On our first Valentine's Day together, my Boaz brought home a rose bouquet with a big heart-shaped balloon. His face was one big smile as he came through our front door after work.

"Happy Valentine's Day!" He gave the bouquet to me with a kiss. I could see how smitten he was with me, grateful for another chance to love and be loved back.

"Thank you so much! Happy Valentine's Day. I love you bunches!" I gave him hugs and kisses. Then I took the bouquet to the kitchen, and put it in a vase of water with the balloon tethered to it.

"Here's yours, Sweetie!" I came up to him as he wrapped an arm around my waist. I gave him a fun card with cute characters with all the things I loved about Boaz.

As he read his card, I noticed tears welling up, "Thank you so much! I really like this." He gave me a big smooch.

Then, I gave him an oversized chocolate kiss.

"Mmmm, I will enjoy this later," he said.

I read his card to me, appreciating his personal love message inside.

As a newly oldlywed couple, we wanted to celebrate the beauty of Christian love as a Twice Blessed couple. He shared that what meant so much to him was having his gifts of love appreciated and displayed, to have love reciprocated once again. I was glad he loved what I had for him, but the card meant far more for him than the chocolate.

Now, as retired oldlyweds, we focus more on demonstrating love through thoughtful, self-designed e-cards and spending quality time together. It's been a learning process understanding what helps each other feel loved, and the time investment has been well worth it.

God has also blessed me that Boaz respects my past marriage with Don and values the insights Don gave me, which we benefit from in our marriage today. I've learned to appreciate his past by acknowledging the pain he endured for so long, as well as some of the joys he experienced before. The blessings of our remarried love is so precious.

***

Leaning back in my chair as I sipped my coffee in reflection, a misty-eyed smile spread across my face as I gazed at that post. *Thank You, Lord, for these precious memories with such a loving, godly man Don was. And thank You for my Boaz, the godly man for whom Don must have prayed to love and care for me in my remaining years. I've indeed been twice blessed.*

THOUGHTS ON THIS CHAPTER

Some of us who have lost our Sweethearts to terminal illness hate looking grief in the face yet again. It's painful, exhausting, and often more than we are willing to endure. We shut it out, pretending holidays like Valentine's Day are just another day. Yet our Lord knows we can't let our mourning fester. He lovingly opens our wounds, cleans them out, and bandages them with His love so we can heal. By His stripes, we are healed indeed.[23] That's why He brings things like colorful holiday decorations and mundane tasks like ordering a headstone to our attention. It is so our tears can bring cleansing to our hearts. Never be afraid to cry.

One way we can participate in our wellness is to remember. Remembering special moments as well as painful one helps turn our mourning into joy.[24] It takes time for this healing to take place. Jesus said, "Blessed are those who mourn, for they shall be comforted."[25] Grief doesn't end; it changes. Be open to allowing God to transform your grief to joy.

I'm not an expert in grief like a mental health professional or pastor. But I am a sister in Christ who has been where you are, and I've been the pastor's wife ministering to women who have lost their Loves. Our stories are very different, yet the same. As you've read my story and worked through the reflection sections to consider your story, I pray that you begin to feel free to live this new life God has given you. May you savor the wonderful memories of your first Love and build upon those new memories with your Second Blessing, the Lord willing.

FOR REFLECTION

Some of the feelings I experienced with transitioning from painful

23   Isaiah 53:5
24   Psalm 30:11; Isaiah 61:3
25   Matthew 5:4 NKJV

grief to joy-filled memories were:

- » Grief Trigger—One of my posts from a few years ago in the "On This Day" at the top of my newsfeed painfully reminded me about a time of intense sorrow shortly after my first husband's death.
- » Denial/avoidance—I had mostly ignored the Valentine's decorations in the local stores. I didn't want to think about it.
- » Remembrance/reminiscing—memories cropped up from my Facebook post. I remembered them like they were yesterday.
- » Wistful reflection—As I reflect on those pain-filled times, I realize how blessed I was for having shared so much love with Don for almost thirty years. Leaning back in my chair as I sipped my coffee in reflection, a misty-eyed smile slowly spread across my face as I gazed at that post.

Questions for Reflection

1. What moments in your love relationship with your First Blessing stand out?

....

....

....

2. Have you shut down your emotions to hide from grief? How long did it last, and what pulled you back to reality?

....

....

....

3. Considering holidays and special events, how do these look now compared to then?

....

....

....

4. If you are married to your Second Blessing, how do you appreciate both Loves? How does your Second Blessing honor your First Blessing? How do you honor his (or her) previous marriage?

Scripture for Reflection

- Romans 5:1–5

- John 16:20–22

- Ecclesiastes 3:4

- 1 Thessalonians 4:13–18

*This chapter is adapted and expanded from "The Last Valentine" from **Life Lessons Learned in God's Classroom**. Permission granted by Kathy Carlton Willis.*

Any other Bible passages or thoughts?

Aknowledgements

B ooks like these take years—yes, *years*—to make it to publication. They also require numerous people behind the author who helped make books like *Twice Blessed* possible. First, I'd like to thank Don Engelhardt, my high school sweetheart now in Heaven, for the incredible thirty years we cherished together. I believe he's smiling down from Heaven as part of that great cloud of witnesses. I'm just sorry he had to suffer so much for so long, but glad he has that spiritual body that will never feel pain or experience illness; it is simply perfect. I'd also like to thank my Boaz, my Second Blessing, who has grown closer into oneness with me—titanium strong. He has supported this work in many ways, leaving me to plink away at my computer in my office for countless hours, and marking up my rough drafts. You are indeed more of a blessing than you will ever know. I'm forever grateful for you!

I'd like to thank my adult children, Seth, Lauren, and Rachel, for helping clarify details, proofreading, and putting up with me all this time talking about this work of love in process. I'd especially like to thank Rachel for using her editing, PR, and marketing skills to help me get this book into the hands of people who have walked through these same struggles with their Sweethearts.

And for all those behind the scenes who helped make *Twice Blessed* a reality. My prayer partners who have prayed for this book for several years, Kathy Carlton Willis, for all her coaching, cheerleading, and editing. Thank you, Michelle Rayburn, for putting up with my brain fog by helping me clean chapters up and making this book a blessing for readers with your keen editing skills, guiding me along the way. For Stella Soto-Crawford at Take Heart Books, for believing in this book, her keen editing eye, and for publishing *Twice Blessed* to bless others who walk this same path. For Emily Gehman and Michelle Chenowyth, their insights and seeing the value of using my story to help others. Thanks to WordWeavers

International and the Ocala chapter for all their input, prayers, and support. Also, I thank many other family members and friends who have trusted God to lead me and encouraged me as I cried, felt like giving up, smiled, and poured my heart out on these pages. I am forever grateful for all of you!

About the Author

Charlaine Martin loves helping women discover God's masterful hand in their everyday life adventures. She is an author, speaker, and Bible teacher whose work has appeared in Faith-filled Family Magazine, Consumer Health Digest, and Crossmap.com. She is also a contributing author in several WordGirls compilations and *Renewed Christmas Blessings* published by FaithLife Creative.

Charlaine has a bachelor's degree in Management with emphases in Christian ministry and exercise science from Malone University (formerly Malone College).

She and her Boaz live in Central Florida. They enjoy putzing the skies in their single-engine plane, cycling on local bike trails, and sharing tickle bugs with their grandchildren.

You can connect with her at www.charlainemartin.com or email her at charlaine_martin@yahoo.com.